searching for Silky

by
Nancy Taylor

Ballast Books, LLC
www.ballastbooks.com

ISBN: 978-1-966786-00-9

Cover Art by Adrian Wilczynski
Cover Design by Mirko Pohle
Interior Illustrations by Ava R. Taylor

"The Writer" from New And Collected Poems by Richard Wilbur.
Copyright© 1947-1953; 1955-1988; Copyright(c) renewed 1975 1996
by Richard Wilbur. Used by permission of HarperCollins Publishers.

Printed in the United States of America

Published by Ballast Books
www.ballastbooks.com

For more information, bulk orders, appearances, or speaking requests,
please email: info@ballastbooks.com

To L. M. L.

"Keep the green tree in your heart—
and the singing bird may come."

Chinese Proverb

Except a living man there is nothing more wonderful than a book! A message to us from . . . human souls we never saw. And yet these arouse us, terrify us, teach us, comfort us, open their hearts to us as brothers.

—Charles Kingsley

I'm thankful for the following people's contributions to this book:

Sisters, Betty and Karen
Parents, Don and Bea
Husband, Russell E. Taylor
Friend Dalsemer
Mrs. Vet
Zackitty Vet (son of Mrs. Vet)
Mr. Bark
Mr. B. R. King
Marya Hahldatter
Ms. B. D. Driver
Mr. Jeffrey Pat D. Drumman
Share Moresun
Mr. Moresun
Miss Polite
Mr. Vet (no relation to Mrs. Vet)
Will B. Vet (son of Mr. Vet)
Mrs. Danas Myth
Cecilya Myth (daughter of Mrs. Myth)
Nelilya Myth (daughter of Mrs. Myth)
Doña Kañuspella
Monamie Géniegékas
Mr. and Mrs. Wish

Thanks also to Frederick, MD, artist Mary Waldhorn, musician Steve Waldhorn, and Dartmouth Professor of English and Creative Writing Melissa Zeiger, for their valuable input.

Illustrations are by Ava R. Taylor (at age five to six). Now, years older, she has graciously agreed to allow her early artwork to be published.

Thank you to my editors Katherine Dixon, Holly Gorman, Kayleigh Rucinski, and Tara Taylor. They have a knack for the expression of beautiful language and for creating a graceful flow of words. The work of these editors enhanced my book and helped to make my message become clear and readable. I am indebted to them, and to all of the team at Ballast Books, for their help and expertise.

Table of Contents

Introduction

Has something seemingly commonplace, even routine, ever captured your attention and fascination—so much so that you find yourself wanting more and more of it? You are fixated on it, even obsessed! It excites you for some reason, a reason that, for the moment anyway, is beyond your grasp, that you can't even imagine.

Well, it happened to me once. This book is about what can happen when you let yourself follow where it leads you, and you end up someplace significant and big, having started with just a little thing, a chance encounter—an ordinary discovery of, say, a kitten!

PART ONE

How the Search Began
—in Six Chapters

CHAPTER 1

The Beginning

Late May 2009

I first laid eyes on Silky as she drowsily fed her four kittens. They lay in a cozy spot in a landscaped garden under a tall, gracious gift-giver of an evergreen tree at the corner of a rural school building. I called the spot Cat Haven. I was working as a music teacher at this school, located in a remarkably lovely setting full of natural beauty. Being surrounded by this semi-wild environment always inspired me and brought me joy. Nature's changing moods, seasonal cycles, a variety of colors—all wonderful.

I might not have noticed this activity in the garden if a colleague hadn't elbowed me during an assembly earlier in the day, informing me that a "local" black cat had borne kittens, and that they were in that particular spot at the front of our building. The word had gone out among many of the children: "Kittens! There are kittens!" Once the magic word was uttered, the children mobilized, providing an open cardboard box and a towel or small blanket for the cat family, as I was soon to see.

I am not fond of cats. I am allergic to them, for one thing. But when I went out to look at those kittens, I found myself transfixed by the mother cat. I was very attracted to, totally enthralled by, this animal. Her bright, piercing eyes piqued my fascination. Until that day, I had never encountered a pair of eyes that could plumb the depths of my soul like that. The cat drew me in, and just like that, I was fervently devoted to her. I could see that this mother cat was a kitten herself. She was small, immature, but gorgeous—sleek and black, with a very small smattering of white hairs on her chest vaguely suggestive of a bib, barely there. Her black kittens were ferocious; they were aggressive, at least one continually attacking one or more of the others. They looked fierce with spare, triangular faces like their mother's. They did not look or act like any kittens I had ever seen.

I visited this charming family whenever I could—I lived close by. I observed them with wonder and delight. I just looked, never touched. I didn't want to interfere with the unfolding of this wild family—feral, as I came to understand. The mother cat wasn't always there, but when she was, I'd see her letting the kittens drink her milk or reclining leisurely nearby under the tall evergreen.

A few days later, I was disconcerted to discover that the tiny kittens were gone. I was especially dismayed as I returned to the campus after lunch a few hours later and saw the mother cat approaching the building; to me, she appeared anxious somehow, concerned even. Now I felt downright sad and upset.

Upon entering the building, I immediately investigated. I learned that a parent of one of the children in the building, a veterinarian, had been alerted to the kitten situation and had taken the kittens away from the evergreen tree to her own home for proper care.

I contacted Mrs. Vet as soon as I was able and expressed my concern. "What about the mother cat?" I asked over the phone. "I feel sorry for her. Isn't she confused, upset, and lonely, worried about her kittens? What can we do for her?" Mrs. Vet answered that the best thing for the mother cat would be to trap her in a cage and bring her in to be inoculated, to have her blood tested for disease, and to be spayed to never have kittens again.

Well. To me, it was a strange and unexpected plan of action. I immediately agreed to do it. We set up a time frame that would be convenient for Mrs. Vet to receive the animal and perform the procedures. I ended the phone call wondering to myself, *I'm supposed to do WHAT now, with a WHAT?!* I would soon find out, first, how to go about it, and second, that it was an appropriate plan, with the blessing of many people and respected animal care facilities knowledgeable about feral cats.

But what to name my magnificent creature? Deep in thought with this quandary, my gaze landed on a container of dairy-free milk left out on the table in front of me. Silk, silken, smooth, satiny, rich, plush. Glossy. *But who would name an animal Glossy?* I thought. That obviously wouldn't work. Then I had it. No looking back: I would call her Silky.

CHAPTER 2

Trapped!

My good friend on whose splendid farm I lived, Mrs. Wish (so-called because Amere Wish is the name of her horse), explained how to go about humanely trapping a feral cat. Basically, I needed to get Silky into a cage. So, I set about it. Inexperienced as I was at this endeavor, for some reason I had absolute confidence that I would succeed. I never doubted that I would have Silky in the cage/trap before long.

Mrs. Wish lent me a nice, big trapping cage and explained how it worked—she had to patiently go over the instructions several times for me. She gave me some baling twine from her barn to keep the trap door open until I was ready to set the trap, and some cat food to use as bait.

A day or two later, we happened to be driving somewhere together in the same car, and we stopped by my workplace so I could show her Cat Haven. She knows a great deal about feral cats, and she said that such a cat would be very happy in that spot because it's sheltered and there are lots of places to hide, what with the different types of shrubs, flowering bushes, ornamental rocks and boulders, and the bird bath.

We circled the parking lot to head for home, and as we passed an old white storage shed with a garbage dumpster enclosure attached to its side, we perceived through the openings in the enclosure (small, broken sections here and there) several black-and-white cats around the dumpsters. Mrs. Wish admired them, remarking that they looked to be handsome, singularly attractive cats. *Hmmph, who are THEY, and what are THEY doing here?* I wondered. *None of them are Silky. I'm sure they don't cross the parking lot into Silky territory (Cat Haven). I'm sure they won't. They're not important,* I thought. Then I promptly forgot all about them.

Per instructions from Mrs. Wish, I established consistent feeding times. I had one at 4:00 a.m. and one at 7:00 p.m., the location being Cat Haven. I simply set out the food and water and then left. It never occurred to me to stay around and watch the food being eaten. Whenever I showed up to set out a feeding, I saw that the food from before had been entirely consumed. I kept up this routine for a week or two and saw nary a cat the entire time. But I ignorantly assumed it was Silky who was eating the food and drinking the water I provided. I believed that I had established an important rhythmic connection between Silky and me. I never actually saw her in this time period. *Was she seeing me?* I wondered.

At first, I set the white Styrofoam plate of food (and the bowl of water) near the cage but not inside it, so that Silky could get used to the cage itself. Then I started placing the food just inside the cage, near the door, to get her used to being inside it. Then I placed the food further and further back in the cage so she might grow accustomed to being well inside the cage. Clever, no? Then I set up a specific day and time to bring the captured Silky to Mrs. Vet. "I will bring Silky to you in a cage early this coming Sunday morning, June 14," I said without a doubt in my mind. "Then you can perform the desired medical procedures." All my focus regarding Silky was on this one goal; I gave no thought as to what might happen with Silky AFTER the medical procedures.

The evening of Saturday, June 13, I was out of town— I use the word "town" loosely—at the wedding of a cousin's daughter. So there was no 7:00 p.m. feeding at Cat Haven. Mrs. Wish had actually recommended skipping the feeding just before the trapping feeding so that the trapee would be very hungry and therefore sure to go for the food inside the cage. So, my absence the night before the planned trapping was actually beneficial to the plan. *Very good*, I thought. *I could enjoy a beautiful, festive, and celebratory family event.*

At 4:00 a.m. on Sunday, June 14, I calmly set the trap. I put food and water and a plastic toy insect (for some fun play time for Silky—this was how foolish my imagination was) at the very back of the cage and removed the baling twine so that upon fully entering the cage, Silky would trip the device, and the cage door would slam shut. Yikes. I went home and set my alarm for close to 7:00 a.m.

I awoke and drove the short distance back to Cat Haven. I knew what I would find, although in reality, there was absolutely no reason to assume this would happen. I was no longer calm. For some reason, I felt that the world around me was coming to an end as I slowly, and with trepidation, walked toward the cage.

Sure enough, when I arrived, I saw a small black cat standing tensely at the very back wall of the cage, as far away from the door as possible, her back against the wall, yellow-orange eyes staring fiercely at me. Her gaze felt threatening, accusing, as if she were thinking, *How COULD you?* I confirmed visually that it was Silky. I was a little scared, but I knew I must proceed.

Mrs. Wish and Mrs. Vet had both recommended covering the cage with a towel for a calming effect on the cat. I made soothing sounds with my voice—probably for my benefit as much as Silky's—as I got closer. As I guided the towel toward the cage, Silky ferociously attacked the cage itself. But as soon as I draped the towel over the cage, she became very still. She never did utter a sound during this entire procedure. It was all very unnerving.

I picked up the cage somehow, and awkwardly carried it to my car. I placed it on the back seat, got in, and called Mrs. Vet to tell her I was on my way. As I drove to her house, following directions I had scribbled onto the back of the program for the wedding ceremony, I sang "Over in the Meadow" to Silky. I also sang a song in Latin, but I don't remember what the song was. (See? Latin comes in handy after all.) I also called Mrs. Wish for moral support. She was impressed with what I had accomplished and very pleased.

I drove with my precious trapee in a stately, dignified manner, drawing out the moment, which I thought suitable to the circumstances. In this way, I ended up at my destination, the nearby home of Mrs. Vet.

CHAPTER 3

~

How So?

Looking back, I realize that I had no concrete way of knowing it was Silky I was methodically luring into the trap/cage. What made me so sure? It didn't occur to me at that time to wonder about that. I simply set the food out at 4:00 a.m. and 7:00 p.m. and then left the scene. I never saw Silky eating the food, so it could have been another cat or cats, or another animal. But the fact is that on that fateful Sunday morning, it *WAS* Silky who ate the 4:00 a.m. meal; I know this—I set out the food at 4:00 a.m. in the cage, I returned at 7:00 a.m., and there was Silky, trapped inside the cage.

I had assumed it was Silky who got each feeding. Was I right about that, or did Silky only happen to get that one (fateful) 4:00 a.m. Sunday morning feeding? What are the chances? Who knows the answer?

I do know now that all of the cats who had been frequenting the old white storage shed area were (are) very quick to detect the location of cat food being set out, even at wide distances from the shed. It doesn't seem possible that only Silky ate that food for the entire time period when I was placing it at Cat Haven (only separated from the old white storage shed by one small parking lot). So how was I so lucky that it was Silky in the cage that Sunday morning?!

CHAPTER 4

Silky So Close to Her Kittens, Yet So Far

As soon as I arrived at Mrs. Vet's house, she placed the caged Silky in the Vet garage, towel over the cage. Silky was being quiet and still. Mrs. Vet asked if I would like to see Silky's four kittens. Thrilled with this invitation, I answered excitedly, "Oh, yes!" She led me into a downstairs bathroom, and there was her young son, letting the four black kittens crawl and tumble all over him. Her son, at that time not the calmest person I knew, was exceedingly patient and peaceful. He was kind to the little creatures. I was introduced to the kittens one at a time, by name: Barny, Smoky, Cooky, and Joe.

The animal-knowledgeable Mrs. Vet was teaching her young son to "gentle," and to domesticate, the wild kittens with a goal of turning them into desirable pets and placing them in people's homes. Thus, he was encouraging them to lie on their backs—a sign of submission—and to learn to trust and love, and not to hurt, humans.

I asked if we could reunite Silky and her "lost" kittens, but Mrs. Vet squelched my idea, pointing out that the kittens had been pretty much weaned by this point. More importantly, she insisted, the four kittens might "regress" and revert to their former wild ways with any more contact with their unrefined, untamed mother. Separation was to be strictly enforced. Thus, one of my fond hopes had been dashed, but in the process, I now had a clearer, more factual picture of the situation. Mrs. Vet suggested that Silky was not even all that interested in being close to her offspring; she probably wasn't missing her brood as much as I had assumed she was.

What were my other hopes for Silky, for her ultimate destiny? I did not know. I suddenly realized I hadn't thought past the point of dropping her off. However, Mrs. Vet had a plan for Silky, and she would carry it out before I could decide what I wanted to do with the cherished object of my affection.

I realized I couldn't hang around Mrs. Vet's house all day, so I left, and that was hard to do. In a bit of a panic, I called a number of people and agencies to get advice on what should be done with a captured feral cat like Silky. Nothing seemed appropriate or doable. I had a feeling I didn't have much time to make up my mind and come up with a plan for Silky so I could call Mrs. Vet to express my desires for, and provide appropriate instructions for, the post-medical care destiny of my beloved animal.

I couldn't have Silky in my tiny house, really, how could I? How would that work? Were pets even allowed in the care-taker's house I was renting on the nearby farm? Should I drive her up to my sister's house in New England, a safe and happy haven for homeless, hapless, beleaguered animals? There wasn't enough time to even investigate, much less carry out, these arrangements.

Sunday afternoon, I contacted a neighbor with a special affinity for wild creatures. This woman had written a book on the subject of wild animals adapting to urban environments. In that book, she had prefaced one of her chapters with a quotation from the "New Sayings of Jesus" discovered during excavations in the ancient city of Oxyrhynchus by Grenfell and Hunt toward the beginning of the twentieth century. The second of the "new" sayings begins with these words: "Jesus saith, Ye ask who are those that draw us to the kingdom, if the kingdom is in Heaven? The fowls of the air, and all beasts that are under the earth or upon the earth, and the fishes of the sea—these are they which draw you." The woman told me that it would be disorienting for Silky to go somewhere other than the outdoor environment with which she was familiar. "Does this cat show an attitude toward being gentled?" she asked.

When I went to bed Sunday night, I had not yet formulated a plan for my Silky, not even close. Monday, I would have to call more people, get more advice from those experienced in such matters, so that I could tell Mrs. Vet what I wanted done with my cat.

CHAPTER 5

What Was Done with Silky After Her Medical Treatment

The next day, I resolved to have a plan for Silky's destiny by that evening. Then, at that point, I would authoritatively advise Mrs. Vet.

But when the evening arrived, I was as baffled about what should be done with Silky as I had been the day before. I called Mrs. Vet. She informed me (authoritatively) that she had released Silky that morning on the campus property from whence she had come, back into the environment with which she was familiar. "Oh," I said.

Before our conversation ended, Mrs. Vet told me that the spaying operation had been successful and that Silky was a healthy animal. Mrs. Vet graciously refused monetary compensation for taking such good and professional care of my wild and wonderful Silky, and that was the end of our conversation.

I had obviously been in no position to determine Silky's destiny, and deep down, I was glad a trusted and capable animal-lover friend like Mrs. Vet had made the move. It was an appropriate, loving, timely, and decisive action. *So be it*, I thought.

The next afternoon, I found out that a certain member of the maintenance team, Mr. Bark, had observed Mrs. Vet's release of Silky onto the campus property he maintained. As happy and excited as I had now become at Silky's prospects, Mr. Bark was just as annoyed and disturbed at Silky's reappearance on the property. "I'd never send a child to our establishment, knowing there were dangerous and savage beasts such as Silky and her sort lurking here," he said. Rightly or not, I felt defensive and saddened by the conversation, and I tried to put it behind me.

CHAPTER 6

Transition to Journal Mode: The Search Begins

For a period of time, thoughts of Silky faded and drifted to the back of my mind. I assumed it would be impossible to get her back, and improbable that I would even catch sight of her again. How would our paths cross? And I felt I certainly could never "have" her the way I thought I wanted to. But I still loved her.

I assumed Silky would be relegated to the status of a precious memory, a cherished recollection of a beloved "four-legged" (to use a Native American term) with whom chance threw me together for a brief time.

My mother said I should write a story about Silky, a suggestion that confounded me, especially coming from my mother. *A story about Silky?* I thought. *What story? I'm not a writer.* What on earth was my mother thinking, urging ME to write a story—about Silky?

The aforementioned Mr. Bark surprised me by relating to me several instances when he thought he had seen "my cat" at various places on the property of our workplace. He seemed to show genuine, kindly interest and respect for my "ownership" of Silky. He seemed to think of her as "Nancy's cat"!

Yes, and at some point as the summer wore on, I started hankering for Silky. I began to miss her—quite badly. *Can I attract her back to me?* I wondered.

Mrs. Wish offered that Silky and I shared a very special bond in spirit, that sometimes a human being and an animal have this kind of relationship, a strong yet invisible connection to one another. I didn't know what in the world she was talking about. But she insisted that Silky and I would definitely meet again. Somehow, we would find each other. Our paths *would* cross in the future. She told me to keep on the look-out and to keep my heart open and seeking for Silky, and then we would surely meet.

I finally decided to try. I began to set out food and water at Cat Haven. I would check the bowls, find that the food had been eaten, and provide new food. For a while, I imagined Silky was eating it. *Hooray*, I thought, *I have a connection with Silky!* Then it dawned on me: What if it was another animal? Perhaps a raccoon. A raccoon dines at night, and a raccoon would eat cat food. Thus the spying period began; I set out the food and then watched to determine what animal was actually eating the food.

If it even occurred to me that Silky was unlikely to return to a site (Cat Haven) where she had been caged, delivered to a "two-legged," then poked and prodded—well, I did not dwell on it. I bumbled forward, not giving much, if any, consideration to this very real possibility.

I decided then to write a story about Silky. I had no idea how the story would unfold. But I did know one thing for sure: Whatever my mother urged me to do was a right and worthy thing to do, a beneficial thing to do, and it behooved me to heed her advice—and to alter my course, if necessary. My mother had always steered me in the right direction.

I decided to begin by recording my observations of my hunt for Silky in a journal. And then I would just see what happened, find out if Silky might lead ME somewhere. In the following pages, I share with you this journal, including my observations, thoughts I had, and pertinent quotations I encountered, in the chronological order (more or less) in which these things occurred.

"The Writer"
by Richard Wilbur

In her room at the prow of the house
Where light breaks, and the windows are tossed with linden,
My daughter is writing a story.

I pause in the stairwell, hearing
From her shut door a commotion of typewriter-keys
Like a chain hauled over a gunwale.

Young as she is, the stuff
Of her life is a great cargo, and some of it heavy:
I wish her a lucky passage.

But now it is she who pauses,
As if to reject my thought and its easy figure.
A stillness greatens, in which

The whole house seems to be thinking,
And then she is at it again with a bunched clamor
Of strokes, and again is silent.

I remember the dazed starling
Which was trapped in that very room, two years ago;
How we stole in, lifted a sash

And retreated, not to affright it;
And how for a helpless hour, through the crack of the door,
We watched the sleek, wild, dark

And iridescent creature
Batter against the brilliance, drop like a glove
To the hard floor, or the desk-top,

And wait then, humped and bloody,
For the wits to try it again; and how our spirits
Rose when, suddenly sure,

It lifted off from a chair-back,
Beating a smooth course for the right window
And clearing the sill of the world.

It is always a matter, my darling,
Of life or death, as I had forgotten. I wish
What I wished you before, but harder.

PART TWO

The Search for Silky:
The Journal

Friday, September 25, 2009

6:45 p.m.
I placed food and fresh water under the tall evergreen tree at Cat Haven. Shortly thereafter, a black cat moved quickly up the small hill at the far end of the curved driveway and onto the grounds of the campus, then disappeared.

7:10 p.m.
I saw several cats—two black, and one black with white boots—at the old white storage shed. One of the blacks stayed in place, stretching and cleaning itself or something. The behavior was very casual. Too far away to see clearly.

Finally, at 7:30 p.m.
One of the blacks (the booted one had gone "inside" to the trash dumpster area) trotted over to the tree, enjoyed the treats, then trotted back to the shed with plenty of pausing to look toward my car (inside of which I sat gazing at the scene).

* * *

Silky has BRIGHT, fiery eyes—yellowish orange.

* * *

The crowd of cats, presumably Silky's crowd, has characteristic and distinctive coloring—featuring black and white. Some of the cats are black. Some of them are mostly black, with white accents: the last third of the tail, for example, or boots, or a bib on the chest. Silky's bib is a small, narrow, faint white patch on her chest.

* * *

They live together, in some sort of colony.

Saturday, September 26, 2009

Raining—no sign of any cats at Cat Haven; no cat walked toward the tall evergreen at the appointed time for food.

Sunday, September 27, 2009

Quite a little group of cats out tonight in the parking lot near Cat Haven as night fell. Where was Silky in this gang? Is this her crowd? One black cat did an amazingly athletic jumping dance—jumping straight up and descending down with paws out as if catching something. A moth? Or toying with something on the pavement. Maybe it was a practice movement for making a capture. Or maybe it was a practice movement for falling safely—upright, on all four paws—from a very high place. For the second time, a black cat appeared from down the road onto the curved driveway shortly after my car pulled into a parking space. A tan, caramel-colored KITTEN was in the group tonight.

Thursday, October 1, 2009

I put the food out slightly later tonight. One black cat (Silky?) approached as usual from underneath a parked yellow bus at the far end of the curved driveway, and one black cat approached from the old white storage shed where the cats live, or at least hang out. After a while, they left Cat Haven one at a time and headed toward the old shed. Did they share the food? There didn't seem to be any squabbling or fighting under the evergreen. Rats! I forgot water.

* * *

A part of Silky's environment is the trash dumpster area next to the old white storage shed abutting the parking lot. Inside this fenced area can be found refuse, discarded food, cardboard, etc. The cat colony loiters there; it's the gang's hang-out.

* * *

Re Silky's clan: they come out into the parking lot of an evening (when all of the school's staff and children have gone home to THEIR homes, and it's quiet) and hang around just outside the white-painted fence around the trash dumpster area. Then ONE goes to the tall evergreen across the parking lot to check out what treats I have put there at Cat Haven.

* * *

Many of these evening behaviors, and the colors, of the parking lot cats are the very same cat behaviors, and colors, described poetically by T. S. Eliot in his "The Song of the Jellicles." Thus Eliot's descriptions—his black-and-white "Jellicle Cats" gathering at night "to practice their airs and graces," waiting for the "Jellicle Moon" to rise, jumping like a jumping jack, caterwauling, as they attend the nightly "Jellicle Ball"—are echoed by my own observations. And all are wearing clean tuxedos to these nightly capers!

* * *

But probably nobody is going to take these cats in. They're too wild, maybe even ferocious now and then, not having been domesticated. As far as I know, they don't hibernate. Therefore, how do they survive? What is their life like?

* * *

These have become exciting times for me, the times when, of an evening, I stare fixedly at the front of the white fence that surrounds the trash dumpster area, and at the white front of the old storage shed, as viewed from my car a distance away, in the parking lot. My eyes strain to discern whether a small, black area on the stark white background is a shadow, a hole at the bottom of the fence, my imagination, or a black cat (and possibly Silky). Is it moving? Yes! It's a cat! Could it be Silky?

I'm enthralled and excited during these times of anticipatory observation. Sitting in a parking lot. Staring at an old shed. By myself. The campus dully quiet and still, devoid of the happy noise and life and camaraderie with which it teems all day long.

Saturday, October 17, 2009

This evening, I tried a new method of getting a little food to . . . Silky? Or to her gang anyway. It's been very cold and rainy for days, and I've been away, not around at the feeding time to put out any food, for about a week. And I didn't want it to get soggy, sitting out. It was still raining, and perhaps the cats needed a little something but didn't want to venture out into the cold rain to get it.

So I pulled my Volvo closer to the storage shed and placed a bowl of food under the yellow bus parked next to it. I called, "Silkeeee, come on, Silky! Silky, Silky, come on, Silky!" I went and sat in my car, waiting.

After a few minutes, a black cat emerged from the hole "doorway" in the fence (a broken part). Silky? It could have been. The cat came out, saw my car, headed back to the hole in the fence, paused to take a second look at my car, and turned around to head back, apparently having sensed that there was no danger.

The cat easily found the food "hidden" under the bus and consumed all of it. Practically no time had elapsed for the food to sit around and lose its freshness. Yay! Ducky! Clearly these cats have keen, sharp senses.

Monday, October 19, 2009

There was a catfight this evening. Yes, at the lovely spot under the evergreen at the corner of the building where I put food out—Cat Haven! Not sure what they were fighting over, since earlier, it seemed that one of the booted cats had snagged the food for itself. There is a grayish cat whose tail is always bushy and who seems to be trouble. This bushy one was there, and that's when the screeching and squalling started. Horrendous sound. A black and a booted cat bolted out of the shrubbery surrounding the tree and sat at a distance. For a while. Then a cat left the scene and joined other cats who were over at the fence around the trash dumpster area next to the storage shed.

Earlier, I had noticed some chasing between a cat and a kitten—maybe even some attacking. There are now kittens in this crowd. Oh my. We've got some rough customers. What will become of this gang?

* * *

In the early days of the search: Oh! Oh! Oh! What is that black patch against the white wall of the storage shed? Is it a shadow? Is it moving? Is it a cat? Is it Silky?

Tuesday, October 20, 2009

All was quiet, sedate, and orderly with the cat population this evening. Shortly after 7:00, four cats filed calmly, single file, into their trash dumpster enclosure from the soccer field. In this order: a booted cat leading, then a black cat, then Bushy, then another black cat. All was then quiet and still. For a long while.

Finally, a black cat ventured out, made its way leisurely across the parking lot, located the food and water I had placed in a new spot with better visibility (for ME), near to the usual one under the evergreen at the front corner of the main building, where my involvement in all of this had started. But the cat only ate part of the food, leaving about two-thirds of it.

Meanwhile, a booted cat exited the storage shed/trash dumpster enclosure and took off in the opposite direction, and ended up running across the soccer field, disappearing into the night.

Monday, October 26, 2009

Not a single cat was to be seen. The area where I observe them was completely devoid of cats. I sat quietly and waited from 7:00 p.m. to 8:00 p.m. I have not been in the habit of calling to them. Their absence was very unusual, a first-time occurrence for me, in fact. Where did they go? I filled the dark-colored, camouflaged bowls under the evergreen at Cat Haven with dry food and water, and went on my way.

Friday, November 13, 2009

This evening, I think Boots hit the jackpot. Here is how his/her windfall occurred. It had been hurricane weather, though mildly. I put out food and fresh water in the usual spot, under the big evergreen at the corner of the main building—Cat Haven. Then I went closer to the cats' residence and put food in a paper bowl underneath a bus nearby and called, "Silkeeee, come on, Silky Silky!" like I had once before. Then I waited in my car. My concern was that even though the rain had finally stopped, the cats in Silky's family might not want to venture out far—perhaps they could duck out, enjoy a meal, then duck back in for the night . . .

After quite a while, Boots came out, sat down, and seemed to quickly sense that food was nearby. Boots made a sure and true beeline for the food under the nearby parked bus, although halting briefly every so often, and consumed all there was in the bowl. Then Boots checked under all the other buses in the parking lot, and also under my car. Amusing! Then this smart little animal headed straight for Cat Haven—Bingo! Possibly a second dinner, because a little while later, a different cat emerged from the Haven.

Incidentally, I had left a cat toy near the cats' residence, for playtime. I found the cat toy soggy and seemingly untouched, ignored.

* * *

I don't feed the feral cats often enough to get them dependent on it. And I don't know if they share the food, or if whichever cat gets there first eats all of it, in one sitting. Visibility for me is poor to nil at Cat Haven, and sometimes I just set out some food and water and then leave, not having time to sit in my car and observe which animals eat it.

* * *

The new feeding spot (location B) is the "post–raining-cats-and-dogs" location. It is underneath a parked bus very close to the cats' residence. As opposed to Cat Haven, under the tall evergreen across the parking lot.

Thursday, November 19, 2009

Today a coworker said to me, "Those cats you saved are doing very well." She was referring to Silky's kittens. She had been to Mrs. Vet's house and had seen two of Silky's kittens there, and they were "playful" and seemed content, well cared for, and presumably domesticated and gentled. However, I'm not the one who "saved" Silky's kittens, am I? 'Twas Mrs. Vet who saved the kittens.

Adapted from the eighth-century writings of Shantideva:

For compassion is the tree that shelters all beings.

It is the universal bridge

That dispels the misty ignorance of the world

And leads the weary traveler out of Samsara into Nirvana.

Mrs. Vet has taught me an effective way to handle, and to actually save, the lives of these wild, feral cats. And her method impressed me with the compassion it demonstrated. As Shantideva has suggested, compassion is key in all things we do, and with all the beings we encounter in our path. The metaphor of the sheltering tree resonated with me because I find it apt, and also because I like to acknowledge the importance, value, and beauty of trees in general. The reader may recall that I actually began this account with a tree—a tall, gracious gift-giver of an evergreen tree.

Tuesday, November 24, 2009

It was dark and drizzling, about 7:00 p.m. As I left the building where I had worked late, I spied Boots sitting on the sidewalk in front of the tall evergreen where I usually place the cat food, waiting patiently. And s/he was staring, his/her eyes fixed on me as I stood by my car. Maybe it was my imagination, but I felt s/he recognized me from quite a distance—as a provider of food, anyway. But I had nothing to offer. After a while, s/he went and checked under the bus near the storage shed where I had twice (only twice, and some time ago) placed food after a long rain (because the cats don't seem to enjoy rain, and I thought they might be hungry after bad weather, and I didn't want them to have to venture out far to get fed). No luck.

I went home to get some cat food (home, about a minute away), came back and did some more work in the building, then reemerged and placed my cat food under the bus. Boots was (still) around. S/he didn't take long at all to find the food under the bus and then enjoy a hearty meal.

How was it that Boots was expecting to be fed by me this night? Had s/he already caught on to my plan to provide food after a long rainy period and place it under the bus? Did s/he now totally "have my number," know my habits, understand what I'm all about, how I think and feel about all of this? S/he seems very aware of the fact that I work so hard at my job that I stay there, at my workplace, well into the evening, usually the last to leave. (I work so constantly and tediously that I'll probably die standing up like an old ox.) Or had s/he been waiting in the likely places every single evening, hoping for the food to come? But I don't put food out every evening. No, much less frequently than that. I get too busy or too tired to crawl under that evergreen tree, clean the black bowls, and then put in new food and fresh bottled water.

I've been obsessively fixated on this gang of feral cats. Now, for the first time (that I'm aware of anyway), one of them is fixated on ME (and my car, too, probably).

But where is Silky?

Wednesday, December 9, 2009

After a cold, wintry, snowy spell, about four cats were out and about on a warmish evening at the appointed hour. When I emerged from working late in the building, one was sitting by the tall evergreen at the corner of the building, as if waiting for something (we all know what). I scrambled around for some cat food and a bowl. Eventually, I placed the food under a parked bus and called, "Silky, Silkeeee! Come on, Silky! Silky! Silky!" As I sat in my car observing, a black cat emerged from the trash dumpster enclosure, located the food quickly, and consumed it. I wondered if it was Silky, my next thought being *I need binoculars*. This cat had a small but very pronounced white patch on the chest and no boots. The presence of this bright, clear white patch, small but big enough to be called a bib, ruled out Silky as being the identity of this cat.

Soon, Boots appeared out of nowhere. Then, lo and behold, a nearly identical cat appeared, seemingly out of thin air; I called this cat Boots as well. Also, a caramel-colored young cat was darting around. Hmmm, what to name this caramel-colored youngster . . . Hmmm . . . Caramel-colored cat . . . Caramel-colored . . . Caramel . . .

When the black-and-white cats see me, they know what comes from me, and they watch my movements closely to determine where I might be placing the food. But only one cat seems to end up eating the food. And it's precious little. How do they survive?

They do know the time, the likely locations, the car, the person, certainly the voice and the call—the cats know what these things mean. Harold Monro's verses float through my mind: "Ho, all you cats in all the street; / Look out, it is the hour of meat: / The little barrow is crawling along, / And the meat-boy growling his fleshy song. / Hurry, Ginger! Hurry, White! / Don't delay to court or fight." And also "(You, domestic Pinkie-Nose, / Keep inside and warm your toes.)"

* * *

Winter, I don't see the cats merely ambling anymore to the parking lot from the old white storage shed and just sitting, bathing themselves, looking around casually. They only look very alert now. They prowl and stalk, or run fast. No trotting. They stare fixedly at something. There is more of a tenseness, and an intentness, in their air.

Thursday, December 17, 2009

Last night, I saw in a dream a cat that was too skinny. I also saw, for real tonight, two cats setting out TOGETHER to hunt. I had not seen THAT before. One of the cats was a black cat. The other was Boots or Snowpatch—I had decided that I couldn't call two different cats the same name, Boots. This really didn't seem right. So one of them is Boots, and the other one is Snowpatch. The problem is, I could never tell them apart, so when I looked at one of them, I didn't know if I was seeing Boots or Snowpatch.

Monday, December 21, 2009

At this point in time, I don't know the status of the feral cat gang at the shed. There has been a major snowstorm. Fifteen inches of snow came down into their neighborhood. That was two days ago, and it's been very cold. I neither saw nor heard any evidence of the cats this evening. No paw prints except some very faint ones heading toward the tall evergreen and vanishing toward the spot. I was painfully aware that the mission evidenced by those paw prints would have been futile . . .

The snow was deep. All entrances to the storage shed underneath which they dwell were blocked with snow, seeming to trap them in if they were, indeed, there. I thought of trying to remove the snow on the side with an ice scraper, but I wondered if that would just let in freezing-cold air. Does the snow cover keep them warm? Do cats dig in the snow? I can't place food under the tall evergreen at the corner of the main building because my footprints would arouse questions and suspicion and lead to discovery of the food dishes. Not a good thing. The administration of the building would frown upon feeding (encouraging) the resident feral cat bunch.

Where in Heaven's name are they? I wondered. *Are they OK? How could they possibly be OK? Oh my, I'm worried about them.*

But I know there is really not much I could, or perhaps should, do for them. They must do their thing. They need to adapt. I can only watch, and feel for them, and give them a handout now and then. I don't want to "enable" them to be poorly skilled hunters and shelter-finders.

And then I thought about the phrase "animal instinct" on which animals, especially wild ones I suppose, rely. The "animal" of "animal instinct" refers to beasts rather than humans, doesn't it? We humans don't have the instincts of animals, do we? So I can (try to) rest content, knowing that the feral cats are guided and protected by their animal instincts, their survival instincts. And by the particular skills and physical features Nature has given to them. I will try not to be anxious or concerned about the well-being of the feral cats.

I comfort myself by remembering Matthew 6:28–29, "Consider the lilies of the field, how they grow; they toil not, neither do they spin: yet I say unto you, that even Solomon in all his glory was not arrayed like one of these . . . O ye of little faith, be not therefore anxious." These words from the Bible reassure me about God's provisions for the natural world.

And thinking of a few bird facts that I happen to know gives me some reassurance about the welfare of the feral cats during the harsh winter months. Birds have amazing survival instincts. For instance, they are gifted weather readers. They know that at some moments, it's best to hunker down for a winter storm, and at other times, it's better to migrate farther south, to "get out of Dodge," where life'll be easier for a while. Also, at harvest time, some types of birds will pick, then bury maybe thousands of acorns for "just in case." And, author Margaret Roach has helpfully pointed out the following bird fact: "If the seed-bearing trees and shrubs of Canada's boreal forests don't produce a sufficient crop, millions of 'winter finches,' who don't normally migrate, rise up and do so, over vast distances." How is that for a Plan B?! The name of Roach's book from which I took the above quote is *And I Shall Have Some Peace There: Trading in the Fast Lane for My Own Dirt Road*. The line she quotes from "The Lake Isle of Innisfree" by William Butler Yeats—"And I shall have some peace there"—speaks to me personally regarding the state of mind I will achieve when I stop worrying about how the feral cats manage to survive in the natural world, with all of its (imagined?) dangers.

But I will admit that it is actually self-serving of me to worry or not worry about the cats' welfare—because this becomes moot when I consider that, as previously mentioned, I could have gotten in trouble with the administration of the campus for feeding these cats; they seem to have a problem with the presence of the feral cats on the property. And I really, really want to avoid clashing with my bosses.

Monday, December 28, 2009

Tonight at the usual time, no sign of the cats. Bitter cold and blustery. I put food under the tall evergreen at the corner of the main building where Silky was settled with her kittens early last Spring. I love this little picturesque spot, and tonight I saw that this pretty, natural haven has become accessible again. I also made a bold and desperate move: I placed two paper food dishes right in front of two of the entrances to the storage shed area. Then I called three times, repeating Silky's name over and over. No cat came out to get food.

After a while I placed those bowls INSIDE the shed area fence (two large gates, loosely connected, form a section of the fence enclosing the trash dumpster area) where the cats could easily reach them. I intended to spirit the bowls away early the next morning before they would be seen by observant custodians who seem to strongly disapprove of feral cat feeding.

Something had been eating the food I had set out for the cats. But exactly what creatures?

I called and called for Silky, but she didn't come—at least not that I could see.

Thursday, January 7, 2010

Finally, with a steady, blasting wind subsiding, the winter cold seemed tolerable tonight, and finally, at the usual evening hour, I saw the cats milling around. They hadn't perished.

Boots or Snowpatch was the most evident. I saw the cat actually go under the parked bus to sit and wait for me to bring the food. But I also saw a cat that I thought was actually Silky—black, with a flash of bright, yellow-orange eyes—as it dashed inside the fenced enclosure upon my approach. So I put a plate of food right outside the opening of worn-away wood where I had seen the possible Silky. I called out. Shortly thereafter, two cats (Boots or Snowpatch from the bus, plus one other, Bushy) gravitated haltingly toward the plate of food. They arrived at the food together. Uh-oh, catfight? No, they both ate peacefully together. The possible Silky ended up with no food from me tonight.

Saturday, January 9, 2010

It was bitter cold again at the early evening hour. I put cat food under the tall corner evergreen tree. I had been putting food there regularly, and it was always completely gone when I would come to check it the next evening. Seemed to me some creature(s), hopefully Silky, had hit it pretty hard lately.

I called for the cat(s): "Silkeeee, come on, girl, Silkeeee, Silkeeeee!" No cat appeared or seemed to be anywhere nearby. I placed more food right outside the dumpster enclosure and waited. No cat came. So I shoved the food and water into the enclosed fenced area, telling myself to remember to remove this evidence of my encouraging-of-wild-animals-near-children crime tomorrow sometime. I saw a falling star, though. The outing was worth it just for that. (Would the cats agree?)

* * *

I have good news and bad news. Good news first: someone said that a particular nearby barn is full of mice. Bad news: I found out that many cats are allergic to corn. I checked the ingredients in the food I've been giving the feral cats, which includes four different flavors—"beef," "chicken," "tantalizing turkey," and "wild Alaskan salmon." And when I checked the ingredient lists, I found that ALL of these foods are mostly, merely, CORN. This is surely inappropriate. Also, cats can be allergic to plastic dishes; their lips and chins could swell up. I learned that it is not even good to feed a cat moist food that comes in a plastic bag.

Yikes. To what allergens or even toxins have I been exposing the cats? I need to make changes to the food and dinnerware, and ASAP—in two shakes of a lamb's tail. I must serve better-quality fare, and on fine china, thank you very much!

Tuesday, January 12, 2010

Today as I was driving, I spied a cat near the road, quite far from the building where I work and where I encounter Silky and her gang. And this was a black cat with a large white "bib" marking and white boots. Sound familiar? This cat had the same markings and coloration as most of the feral cats who frequent my workplace. But this cat was a couple of miles from Silky's gang's residence—almost in the next town. Was this a feral cat? Where did s/he come from? Was s/he one of our gang? The main thing is that it wasn't Silky; I felt pretty sure of that.

Would I recognize Silky if I saw her now, eight months or so after I humane-captured her as a young mother to have her spayed, tested for disease, and inoculated? How much bigger would she be by now? Have her distinctive markings changed? Would I know her? I wasn't sure.

* * *

Here is a hint for those who would like to cover up their boot-prints in the snow: don't go back and stamp or rub them out with your own boots. It doesn't work; you just end up leaving more bootprints. Instead, go back and "wipe" them away with a stick or other implement as you move backward along the path your bootprints made. Et voila!

Sometime later in January of 2010

I filled the brand-new, dark-colored bowl (Kosta Boda crystal no less) under the tall evergreen—with GOOD food from now on, with no corn filler—and then I saw what looked like a circular dark spot, or maybe a puddle, on the sidewalk nearby.

I knew there should be nothing there. What was this circular black area? It turns out it was a caramel-colored striped cat disguised as a puddle!

As I emerged and surprised him/her, s/he got scared and bolted for the storage shed but stopped halfway there to see if the food area was still dangerous. I had faded back into the background, so this cat made a U-turn, headed back to the tree, and enjoyed a meal. Another cat sat by the old shed watching all of this.

* * *

I read in *Time* magazine's "Verbatim" section a quotation by a woman who, while strolling down a street one day, encountered a cat, dropped the cat into a wheelie dumpster bin, closed the top lid, and then immediately walked away. (The cat, named Lola, survived after spending fifteen hours in the trash bin.) An online video that showed her dumping the cat earned this lady much hateful criticism, angry disparagement, even death threats. Her response: "It's just a cat, at the end of the day."

Monday, February 1, 2010

I arrived at the parking lot at 7:15 p.m. with some cat food. Boots or Snowpatch was sitting by a parked bus and saw me pull in. I loaded a paper bowl with a can's worth of "wet" food. Very unusual treat from me, but when I'm eyeballing them, I feel OK about giving them wet food, as it won't sit around for long and either freeze in the winter or go bad in the summer. I placed it at the entrance to the dumpster area at the old shed, near one of the "cat doorways." (A bottom portion of the wooden fence was missing, broken off, and made just the right-sized entryway for a cat.) As I did so, an animal just inside was obviously startled, and some crashing sounds ensued. I called, "Silkeee, come on, Silky!" Boots or Snowpatch—often the first to get the food—headed for the bowl and started eating.

Was the food eventually shared? I hope so. I saw another cat hanging around outside the enclosure. I believe it was Bushy. I placed dry food under the tall evergreen, and when I came back, the paper bowl had disappeared from view, so I couldn't check to see if the present cats had taken all of the food. To where do the paper bowls travel when I feed the cats in this way? They don't leave the paper bowls where I place them; the bowls end up somewhere else. I wondered about that.

I saw at least one cat sitting outside the fence, bathing him/herself. In the freezing cold! I think they do that after they have enjoyed a meal. I still don't know much about cats.

* * *

Bowl found. It's only paper after all, and it probably scoots around as the cats eat. Anyway, I removed this "evidence" of my clandestine activities in a timely manner, before it could draw notice and suspicion from any "two-leggeds."

* * *

Paw prints around the tall evergreen. Lots of them. This is the tree of Cat Haven. It is a tree of life, of shelter. It has roots deep into Mother Earth, and its crown soars up to Father Sky.

Trees provide benefits and gifts for us, and people have their own concepts about what those gifts are. For instance, consider how the shade trees of "shadetree mechanics" have helped heavy automotive work to get done. These large, stalwart trees have lent a strong arm on which to hoist up items as heavy as a car engine! My husband, who lives across the river, is a talented, dedicated automotive engineer, and he refers to the mechanics' shade tree as "a thing to do work—to accomplish work."

And what about "trail trees"? Wounded and forced to grow at an impossible angle in order to indicate a significant direction of travel, those trees must surely be the living vestiges of civilizations or cultures earlier than ours. Native Americans could cleverly contort a young tree in a manner like this: they would take a sapling (usually a white or red oak), bend it over, and cut off the main stem just above one of the branches so that the branch would actually become the new trunk. They would tie down the sapling to a stake until its new form became "set." The wound at the resulting "elbow" would form a sort of knob that would point in the desired direction. Taken together, in a sequence, some would seem to form actual routes, so maybe these trees are a navigational system. Or a particular tree seems to point out a specific destination—to guide a woodsman toward water, safety, or a food supply, perhaps.

Traditionally, May Day (celebrated on or around May 1) is an honoring of Nature, the natural world, the return of long days of sunshine, and especially of flowers and the new growth of vegetation that occurs in spring. All of my students know and sing the May Day Carol, which refers to the age-old custom of presenting beloved people with a "branch of May," described in the carol this way:

I've been a-wanderin' all this night and the best
part of the day,
But when I come back home again I will bring you
a branch of May.

A branch of May I bring you here, and at your
door I stand.
It's nothing but a sprout, but it's well budded out
by the work of God's own hand.

What an amazing gift—those marvelous buds showing such
promise, fresh beauty, and hope. When my students get
together for May Day, the youngest children sing a song called
"I'm a Little Flower" while acting out a growing flower. We
sing "The Rattlin' Bog," which celebrates the tree and the life-
forms that the tree supports, including birds in their nests. This
song honors every part of the tree in turn, a well-known and
often sung "celebration of the tree and the life cycle" song.

There is a paragraph in Charles Frazier's *Nightwoods* that
vividly describes the gift-giving nature of trees—in particular,
fruit-bearing orchard trees. The novel's heroine observes that
these trees behave "more rationally than vegetables," that they
are "slow and careful." Frazier goes on to say the following:

> These had been let go for decades, and the limbs had
> grown criss-crossed and shaggy with dun-colored
> moss and lichen, yet they still made about as many
> fuzzy peaches in summer and bright speckled apples
> in fall as she could eat, whether fresh or dried in
> brown leathery rings or canned. Even without prun-
> ing and fertilizing, the elderly trees would probably
> go on for at least one person's little lifetime, offering
> themselves forward against the uncertain future with
> grim persistence.[1]

---

[1] Charles Frazier, Nightwoods (New York: Random House, 2011).

Friday, February 9, 2010

Cat Haven under the huge evergreen is messed up these days. The recent storm—a.k.a. the Double Blizzard of 2010— dumped at least two feet of snow and broke a large, low-hanging branch of the evergreen, dropping it down onto the feeding area. Deep snow and debris have made entry impossible for me. The cats have still looked for food there, though, on these windy, wintry nights. Paw prints are everywhere. When they spotted me last night, the cats made a beeline for Cat Haven, but alas, to no avail. There was nothing there for them to eat. It made me sad to see their hopes dashed, to know that Cat Haven had failed them.

For now, I must set out the food at the old shed's trash enclosure at the far edge of the parking lot for convenience's sake. So tonight, I stopped by there. As expected, Boots or Snowpatch quickly showed; Boots (or Snowpatch) seems to take the most advantage of what I have to offer, which is really precious little, but it's something. This cat was black with white markings, including four boots and a big, white "bib" on its chest—one of two colored like that.

Boots or Snowpatch briskly climbed to the top of a huge snow pile (before I could prepare the items necessary to serve food) to get a better view of the surrounding area and check what might be going on and where I, food giver, might be located. The snow doesn't seem to unduly faze the cats; they do go out into it. The cat tried keenly to keep track of my whereabouts.

I set out food and water at the trash enclosure and I watched, teeth chattering like a woodpecker with palsy, as Boots or Snowpatch feasted. Then Bushy raced over, so I had to refill. I drove away to run an errand, then came back to collect the empty paper bowls ("evidence"). As I was driving away, a plain black cat appeared. Silky? Tired and cold as I was, anxious to get home, I had to set out a new bowlful of food. The possible Silky approached the other cats, tail puffed up, and ate steadily and in peace, with Bushy eating now and then from the same bowl. The cats can (and do) share nicely.

Sunday, February 21, 2010

I attended a service at the very small, old, and venerable church nearby. A children's leader gathered the youngest worshippers present in church this day and distributed birdseed to them. The leader referred to a passage from the Bible—"The Sermon on the Mount." The particular quote used from this astonishing section of speech was:

> Therefore I say unto you, Take no thought for your life, what ye shall eat, or what ye shall drink; nor yet for your body, what ye shall put on. Is not the life more than meat, and the body than raiment? Behold the fowls of the air: for they sow not, neither do they reap, nor gather into barns; yet your heavenly Father feedeth them. Are ye not much better than they? Which of you by taking thought can add one cubit unto his stature?[2]

The children's leader gently suggested to the girls and boys that "God would like help with this," pointing out that "The

---

[2] Matthew 6:25–34 (King James Version).

deep snow covers sources of food for the birds." I would interpret this Bible passage differently: The message I took from it
was to put total trust in God and stop worrying. But I couldn't
help but applaud anyone's attempt to engender a spirit of sym-
pathy, kindness, and helpfulness toward animals. I think that's
important. It's a positive trait in humans. And to children's
credit, they, in particular, seem to be made happy by tending
to the welfare of animals.

This little lesson in church obviously added to my ambiva-
lence about feeding Silky and the local feral cat population.
The Bible makes clear the love of God for animals and the
importance of them. And yet passages like this one seem to
instruct that we leave the wild ones to their own devices and
not worry about reaching out to them at all. But I include it
because I feel it is worth pondering, turning over in the mind.
There needs to be freedom in interpretation of the Bible,
which gets us thinking, reading, taking it all to heart. I think
everyone can agree that this is a deep but lovely (and lively)
issue to contemplate.

* * *

There is so much we don't know. We're lucky if we can even
guess at various aspects of other people's and animals' lives.
Let's face it: I may never know what happened to Silky. I have
no way of knowing. We are not all-seeing, all-knowing, and
all-understanding creatures. Any vehicle—even my own—
could have run over Silky by now, and I might never know it.
I will probably never know her fate. This thought is a source of
sadness to me.

Monday, February 22, 2010

Tonight there was a cold, gentle rain. I went with the rain plan (location B), and the cats caught on quickly. I placed food under a bus parked near the shed where they dwell, then called, "Silkeee, come on, Silky! Silky, Silky!" Shortly after, Boots or Snowpatch emerged from the enclosure at the shed and headed right for the food. Two other cats arrived later from parts unknown.

I trained my car headlights on the scene, and the cats didn't react to that at all; they didn't mind the bright lights one bit. They do look alarmed and on high alert at the slightest SOUND, though. I saw Caramel, Boots, and Snowpatch contentedly sharing the little bowl of food. No Silky. They lingered under the bus for a while, milling around under there and bathing themselves with their tongues. Boots or Snowpatch kept watching me intently. Finally, one at a time, they dived back under the fence enclosure into their dwelling place (which is actually UNDER the adjacent white storage shed, I think).

They look fine and healthy—strong and lean, with nice fur coats—but not because of me, of course. All I can manage is a small quantity of decent food now and then, with some fresh water.

Friday, February 26, 2010

Lots of cats had something to eat this freezing, snowy night. I placed a bowlful under a parked bus, utilizing location B for nights with precipitation, knowing that the cats had caught on to location B long ago. I called, "Silkee, come on,

Silky, come on, girl!" After a moment, the first cat to emerge from the shed was either Silky herself or a black cat resembling Silky! I couldn't get a good look at the cat to detect the color and nature of its eyes or to look for Silky's subtle white marking, which is nearly nonexistent—for all intents and purposes, Silky looks like a black cat. After s/he froze for a moment when s/he saw me standing nearby, s/he headed straight for the food, soon to be joined by Caramel. As the two cats finished, Boots or Snowpatch appeared, so I had to produce another bowlful of food. Then Boots joined Snowpatch, or Snowpatch joined Boots. And as they finished, more cats approached, so I went back for yet another bowlful. I also provided a bowl of fresh water.

Several more cats appeared from all directions. They were just suddenly THERE, seeming to materialize out of thin air. I felt I had to keep producing new bowls of food because I couldn't bear to see any of the cats disappointed, having arrived on the scene only to find empty bowls. The cats, between them, ate every morsel and shared nicely with each other. Neither fighting nor hogging. Most of them lingered under the bus, bathing themselves and being friendly with each other.

The one that I thought might be Silky approached my car to check under THERE for food. This was the only cat to explore possibilities outside the bus location. If it WAS Silky, she had grown since last year, looking bigger and more mature—very beautiful, in fact. She was so young when I first saw her almost a year ago feeding her four black kittens with tiny white markings on their chests: Barny, Smoky, Cooky, and Joe.

Wednesday, March 3, 2010

Nick Bottom, a beloved Shakespeare character in *A Midsummer Night's Dream*, underwent a wacky transformation at the hands of the mischievous magician-elf Puck, in which his head was suddenly changed into that of a gross and boorish donkey. His friends bolted in horror, and the bewitched, braying Bottom wandered away, to be MIA indefinitely. His friends, mystified and sorrowful, tried to carry on without him, even though he had been a strong and bold leader to them in many ways, inspiring them all to greater heights. Perhaps they wondered if they had lost him forever.

After a period of time, Puck mercifully released Bottom from the spell. Bottom found his way out of the woods in which he had dwelled in his enchanted state and headed for home. One of his friends, Peter Quince, noticing Bottom's approach, cried out excitedly, "Bottom! O most courageous day! O most happy hour!" and a joyful reunion took place.

Quince's eloquent exclamation of delight at the reappearance of Bottom captures well my joyful, jubilant feeling when I finally found myself face-to-face with Silky one March afternoon. It was a thrill! I was overjoyed with the presence of Silky at last.

Yes, I found Silky on this day. Or rather she found me. Here is how she did it. Yesterday, as I walked on the sidewalk by Cat Haven, I sensed that a black cat was sitting there in the shadows under the huge evergreen, but it was too early for the cats to be looking for me with my pitiful little bowl of food—only 4:30 or 5:00, and broad daylight. Yet a cat WAS there, waiting and watching quietly. I backed up and looked closer, and yes, it was a black cat, and the cat had moved into a more exposed position.

Our eyes met. They were Silky's fiery yellow-orange eyes. I spoke to her, and we silently communicated our vibes to one another, but I could not offer any food because people were around to notice. So I said "Goodbye," and that had to be that.

Today at around 5:00, as I walked by the Cat Haven corner, trying to get a few more things done at work before I would head home, I spotted the black cat again. But this time the cat ran away, toward the reception area of the building. A bit later, as I entered the building using the door nearest to Cat Haven, I looked across the wide walkway entry area— toward the left-hand side of the front garden—and there was Silky, sitting up in the branches of a sturdy holly bush right at the edge of the concrete. Our eyes met once again, and I checked out the tiny white patch on her chest, confirming that it was Silky. I spoke to her for a long time because now I wanted her to have as long a time as possible to learn definitively the sound of my voice, and especially to securely grasp the love and care it conveyed. I wanted her to associate my voice with forthcoming treats and gentle, kindly, nourishing actions toward her.

I went and got a bowl of wet cat food—turkey-flavored, with GRAVY—and set it near the base of the holly bush. I called softly, "Silkeee, come on, girl, here's your food, come on . . ." She kept staring at me. I rattled the branch near the dish (as if I really needed to draw attention to the food near her) and then went to my car to observe. She started eating the food. Satisfied, I went back inside to do more work.

I came out to check on the situation and found Caramel eating Silky's food! I was angry at first, but then I told myself that perhaps, in a way, it was actually these other cats that were responsible for getting Silky and me back together, so I should be glad for them. Caramel fled when I appeared, but the bowl was now empty anyway. I went away for a while but wondered how much food Silky had gotten for herself before ol' Caramel showed up.

When I came by again, and I peeked at the holly bush, there was Silky again—waiting, it seemed. We stared at one another, her gaze penetrating, riveting, steady. Then I told her not to go away, that I would be back soon. Surely superfluous comments, unnecessary things to say to Silky. Because by now, Silky, intelligent and also bent on survival, must have made the connection between my presence and sustenance. I came back with a paper bowl of fresh water and a paper bowl of dried cat treats. I set them under the holly bush, and this time I stayed nearby to observe more closely. Silky came to the food and water and ate and drank eagerly, cleaning up all the food in the bowl. And this time she went on her way afterward, soon gone from the scene entirely—as I noted when I checked a few times before finally going home.

So Silky was the real winner of the feeding today, the honor shared only at a distant second place with Caramel. She grabbed my attention EARLY, way ahead of the usual cats (Boots, etc.), and made it clear what she wanted from me, and of COURSE I complied. She stayed hidden, undercover, camouflaged cleverly among low, thick bush branches, but in places where she knew I would find her.

I want her to be happy and to have a good, comfortable, rich life, free of disease, free of fatigue from having kittens all the time (I DID see to that). Now, maybe I could continue observing her and confirming her well-being. That's my goal. My feeling during the afterglow of my long-awaited reunion with Silky is well expressed in the last line of "Pippa's Song," a poem by Robert Browning: "All's right with the world."

That line kept coming into my head. Yes, all's right with the world.

* * *

"Pippa's Song" from *Pippa Passes*, a long dramatic poem/play by Robert Browning:

> The year's at the spring
> And day's at the morn;
> Morning's at seven;
> The hillside's dew-pearled;
> The lark's on the wing;
> The snail's on the thorn;
> God's in his heaven—
> All's right with the world.

* * *

Silky is not very big, could not be described as a "large" cat. She is rather small but not thin.

Thursday, March 4, 2010
Friday, March 5, 2010
Sunday, March 7, 2010

I looked for Silky but didn't see her. I ended up giving some food to Caramel (who is looking sort of fat these days) on

Thursday and to an unknown cat on Friday. By late Sunday night, the cats had been left to their own devices for the weekend. In fact, more often than not, they are left to their own wiles and skills to find food and water. I'm too busy and/or too tired to supply the cats with food every evening. There's no way I can make that happen. No spring chicken, I now live in a rather slow and creaky old body. Therefore, many nights go by when I do nothing to tend to the feral cats. It is what it is, and maybe it's actually for the best.

Their attitude in general toward the humans of all ages at my workplace is this: They are shy and wary, they avoid, and they keep their distance. They are rarely observable during the workday, even though they (seem to) live right there at the site, by our side. They tend to hide. But not so much around me, since they have become used to my interactions with them, and they know that my presence means chow.

Tuesday, March 9, 2010

On the way to choir practice this evening, I was shocked by the sight of Boots or Snowpatch lying dead at the side of the road in front of my workplace, apparently struck down by a passing vehicle. The strong, handsome, noble, self-assured Boots or Snowpatch, one of the ever-present stalwarts, one of those who always led the way, will grace the parking lot no longer with his or her gallant, majestic presence.

As soon as I got home after choir, I called the authorities and gave them the location of the cat lying by the side of the road, and they simply answered, "We'll see what we can do." I had no idea what would happen to the remains of Boots or Snowpatch, and when it might happen. I prayed, "May God have mercy, and may gentleness and due respect be shown."

Later on in the night, with the death of Boots or Snowpatch very much on my mind, I got a feeling of deep peace and calm contentment. It was lovely. My usual anxieties, tenseness, and sense of rush, and all the doubting just disappeared. I heard again the words from "Pippa's Song," Browning's poem: "God's in his heaven, all's right with the world," just as I had thought of this poem when I was overjoyed at reconnecting with the very-much-alive Silky. It was strange and unexpected and incomprehensible as to why I should be visited by this wonderful, powerful feeling at that particular time. I didn't understand it at all.

Also in the aftermath of my sad discovery of Boots or Snowpatch's demise, I kept hearing the words to a duet I had sung at choir practice this evening: "It won't be long 'til we'll be leaving here. Any day now, we'll be going home."

Thursday, March 11, 2010

This morning, I contacted local authorities, for the second time, to come and pick up the remains of Boots or Snowpatch, still lying at the side of the road. An hour later, a friendly man from the Humane Society showed up in a white van with flashing lights and produced several plastic bags. He told me that Boots or Snowpatch would be examined for a "chip" that might be embedded inside him/her, with information about his/her background, owner, and home. I said that probably wouldn't be necessary in this particular case. His reply was that it is the Humane Society's policy, always done with "domestic type" animals they find. This seemed like a good thing.

The fellow did a nice, careful job with Boots or Snowpatch. He thoughtfully arranged and left behind in the cat's place of death a couple of bright yellow daffodils in tinfoil that a coworker of mine had placed with the fallen s/hero earlier in the day.

Sunday, March 21, 2010

I don't know how long Boots or Snowpatch had been lying there before Tuesday evening, March 9, when s/he was spotted by me. We can't ever really know a whole lot; we just don't know, but we move forward anyway, albeit blindly.

* * *

In Kenneth Grahame's *Wind in the Willows*, the hero, Mole, during his long wanderings far and wide with his pal Rat, suddenly receives the summons of "Home," or "Dulce Domum" as Grahame puts it. In other words, he sensed that his little tunnel home was nearby, not far away, within reach. This sudden "mysterious fairy call from out the void," the book says, "took him like an electric shock," and Mole felt compelled to obey it instantly. So Rat and Mole headed for Mole's home together.

They reached Mole's house in a timely fashion because despite the fact that moles are generally considered to be "blind" (What does "blind" REALLY mean?), they were unerringly and sure-footedly guided by the signal that Mole had received. There, they scraped together a meal from bits of leftovers tucked away in various cupboards and drawers, including several bottles of beer found in the cellar. The evening was topped off by a visit from Mole's friends, the fieldmice, who, caroling that evening, gathered in Mole's forecourt in order to serenade him.

In the final verse of the mice's carol "Villagers All," Grahame reminds us of a compelling and beloved aspect of this legend of a divine stable birth, which is that the beasts of the barn surrounded their manger and warmly attended the newborn with loving care. Another way to put it is to use Grahame's wonderful idea: <u>Animals</u> were the first to declare Noel!

Regarding the invisible signals animals pick up, such as the one Mole had received through his senses that told him *"Home!"* Grahame writes:

> We others, who have long lost the more subtle of the physical senses, have not even proper terms to express an animal's intercommunications with his surroundings, living or otherwise, and have only the word "smell," for instance, to include the whole range of delicate thrills which murmur in the nose of the animal night and day, summoning, warning, inciting, repelling.[3]

* * *

I wonder where Silky is right now.

* * *

> For the animals shall not be measured by man. In a world older and more complete than ours they move finished and complete, gifted with extensions of the senses we have lost or never attained, living by voices we shall never hear. They are not brethren, they are

---

[3] Kenneth Grahame, The Wind in the Willows (London: Methuen and Company, 1908).

not underlings, they are other nations, caught with ourselves in the net of life and time, fellow prisoners of the splendour and travail of the earth.[4]

* * *

Prior to my initial encounter with Silky and my subsequent enthrallment with her, I was not interested in cats and didn't care to know anything about them. How things have changed! But I'm basically just interested in *one* cat—Silky.

Sunday, March 21, 2010 (continued)

I remember clearly my last encounter with Silky. She ended up in a position to be face-to-face with me, but she looked tense, even terrified. Ready to bolt or attack—on high alert. I've been mulling over this aspect of Silky's attitude during the meeting because I've been troubled, bothered by it. It's obviously not how I would like Silky to feel toward me. But at least she remembered where she might get food, and she overcame her fears enough to find the right person at the right place—even in broad daylight and with other people milling around.

Tonight, as I arrived in the parking lot at 8:00, Caramel was waiting. Caramel got all the food and water; no other cat was in sight. Caramel was meowing at me—and long, plaintive meowing it was too. S/he hung around the bowls, as if (perhaps) guarding the little bit that was left that s/he couldn't finish. It seemed so precious to this cat. Finally, it was high time that I left, so I had to take the remains and throw them away—evidence, remember?

---

[4] Henry Beston, *The Outermost House* (Garden City, NY: Doubleday, Doran and Company, 1928).

The tall evergreen at Cat Haven is not a good location for cat feeding these days. A huge limb is broken down from the aforementioned Double Blizzard of 2010. Someone might try to work on the tree, and then the glass bowls would be discovered. As I've mentioned, feeding the feral cats is frowned upon on this campus, a no-no. I need a plan C.

Aha! I realize now that Silky herself has established it. The holly bush is now officially location C.

Friday, March 26, 2010

The other night, I saw Boots or Snowpatch sitting quietly by the old white storage shed.

* * *

I learned from someone in our community that Cooky has a house in which to live—a happy home with a roof and people to love him or her, meet the needs of this offspring of Silky, and take good care of him/her. S/he has been given a new name: Itty Bitty. And apparently, s/he is on the small side and has recently developed a couple of white markings on the feet—boots! S/he has a tiny, faint "bib" or chest patch of white. All else is black.

* * *

Yesterday afternoon, I placed a wooden salad bowl full of cat food under the large holly bush near the front wall of the building, at the entryway where I had encountered Silky. Behold, location C, launched! The only cats who had been fed there were Silky and Caramel. I could now check on the contents of the bowl easily and handily, by just looking out a huge front window. Easy. Duck soup. The bowl is dark-colored and blends in with the surroundings, and thus I hope no one sees it but me. It is also very easy for me to reach.

This morning, I saw that the bowl was empty. What animal got the food? What cat? Silky? That was, and is, my fond hope.

* * *

Apparently, the father in the family that now owns Cooky doesn't like Cooky. When Cooky first came into their household, the man took an immediate dislike to this kitten of Silky. A family vote was called for as to whether the little creature could stay or not. The father was outvoted by everyone else, so Cooky stayed.

* * *

This morning, a little boy who comes to the building every day said that "all black cats are wild and fierce" or something to that effect; he may have even said "wicked" or "evil." I questioned the veracity of this statement, but he would only back off a little bit by saying, "Well, MOST black cats are that way." He seemed so sure of this. What on earth could he possibly mean by this, and why would he think such a thing?

Friday, March 26, 2010 (continued)

Tonight, Caramel was sitting quietly by the storage shed when I arrived at the parking lot with cat food at the ready. Caramel got first shot at the paper bowls, even after I had called, "Silkeeee, come on, Silky!" thereby luring out a large black cat who didn't seem to want to share the small bowl with Caramel. I placed another bowlful nearby for the large black cat, but Caramel was, for some reason, the first to get at that bowl as well. The large black cat was doomed to be the finisher. Eventually, the black cat and Caramel went back to the first bowl of food and shared what was left.

A little later on, the large black cat crossed the parking lot, stopping now and then to size things up or to stare at me and to determine my whereabouts. S/he didn't even bother to go up the small rise to Cat Haven to check for food. Instead, s/he rounded the corner and seemed headed for the holly bush—the brand-new location C. I don't know if s/he got to the wooden salad bowl of food or not. I was, er, "prevented" from investigating that: I didn't want to scare the cleaning ladies again. From now on, I will call this large black cat Gen-gi, for "gentle giant."

The cats know me, and they seem to know my various cars. Even though they would never want to be touched by me, or even be very close to me, they do accept my presence, and they are very observant of and interested in my movements (for obvious reasons).

N. B.—The trash is brought out to the old storage/trash shed these days at about 8:30 p.m. by the cleaning ladies. Must keep in mind.

Saturday, March 27, 2010

I went at night (9:45) to try to find Silky. Caramel was waiting just outside the shed. I set out a paper bowl of food, and Caramel got it, of course, to be briefly joined by Gen-gi and Boots or Snowpatch.

I drove around the corner of the parking lot to park and refill the wooden bowl at location C. As I was arranging food and water bowls, I heard the sound of an animal at the other side of the fat holly bush. I finished setting up the food, and as I went around one side of the huge bush to go to my car, a cat dashed around the other side to get to the food that s/he knew was there. I felt fairly certain that it was a smallish black cat that I had glimpsed.

I waited in my car, and after a while, the cat moved to the near side of the holly bush and sat there in the dark, watching me. I stared back, thinking to myself that it was Silky and that we could reconnect and communicate with each other, if even from a distance. Finally, the cat moved briskly but stealthily, keeping a low profile, across the wide, lighted concrete entry area toward Cat Haven (location A) and climbed on top of the birdbath and perched there. Caramel.

Saturday, April 3, 2010

For the past few feedings (ever searching for Silky), the only cat to get the food and eat it has been Caramel. Early or late, s/he is there waiting for me or appears shortly after I start arranging the food and water. Even if I hide my activities from the cat home (i.e., the old white storage/trash shed), s/he appears soon after I start getting the bowls cleaned and ready. S/he isn't afraid to get as close as four feet from me. S/he darts to and fro impatiently as s/he keeps an eye on the developing food situation. S/he will even meow at me; the other cats don't do that at all. S/he has me all figured out, and as a result, no other cats are receiving any of the food from me, least of all Silky (who has a completely different modus operandi). Caramel is the only cat I have seen in quite a while.

* * *

I read this quotation in *Time* magazine's "Verbatim" section, words spoken by a lieutenant governor of South Carolina and Republican gubernatorial candidate: "My grandmother was not a highly educated woman, but she told me as a small child to quit feeding stray animals. You know why? Because they breed." *Time* reported that he said these words while criticizing policies that extend welfare benefits to poor, destitute people.

"Because they breed". . . What a shocking new angle to consider on the issue of whether or not to feed strays. I include this quotation because I would like to demonstrate the fact that a wide variety of opinions exist concerning the feeding of stray, or feral, animals. Well. I must refuse to even consider this one at all, seeing as how the statement shows such an appalling lack of sensitivity, wisdom, understanding, and empathy. And the fact that this politician equates impoverished people to stray animals causing problems by "breeding" is so patently offensive that I will not dignify it with discussion.

* * *

"Initiative" is one of the Virtues of the Month at the establishment where I work. Should we give feral cats handouts? Do they show enough initiative, or should we force them to use more initiative or show more motivation?

Yes, they surely do show initiative, must be almost constantly doing so. I can't imagine what they face, what challenges them every moment of every day. They have so little with which to work.

Monday, April 5, 2010

Tonight, Caramel and Gen-gi consumed the food and some of the water I put out for Silky. Gen-gi can't be Silky; Gen-gi is a big cat with a faint but larger GRAYISH-white patch on the chest. I think Gen-gi might be an old cat. Gen-gi is either less ravenously hungry than Caramel or is afraid to anger Caramel over which of them gets to eat the food. Gen-gi SEEMS a little less interested or less alert regarding the food. So I took it upon myself to put out another bowl of food at a distance from Caramel and the first bowl. Caramel ran right over to the new bowl.

At first, Caramel did challenge Gen-gi when Gen-gi approached the first bowl of food from across the parking lot. Caramel took a "stance" right in Gen-gi's face, so to speak. But then they both worked things out, and each got some food, but I believe Caramel got the lion's share. Eventually, both cats ate together peacefully and seemed satisfied. There was calm bathing afterward.

* * *

I like to observe the other local cats in the parking lot gang, but I'm only interested in them as a kind of backdrop in front of which Silky can be featured. Why am I fascinated by this one particular creature? Does she call forth in my mind something abstract but desirable, something I need? Perhaps Silky represents "inspiration" to me. She seems to be the embodiment of inspiration—elusive, hard to grab and keep hold of, strong, focused, and focusing, unpredictable as to when the visitation will happen, appearing out of nowhere, but coming on in a striking and welcome "flash" that seizes your complete attention. Like a stroke of genius. Something to at least TRY to foster and encourage.

* * *

Victor Hugo expressed this thought: "Inspiration and genius—one and the same." So if Silky represents inspiration, then she would also represent genius, according to Hugo. She does manifest herself, in my life anyway, like a stroke of genius, with suddenness and with an aura of brilliance—and not very often.

Silky, where are you?

Tuesday, April 27, 2010

My cat-feeding excursions to the parking lot have been sporadic lately, and I have shown up at irregular hours. But every time, one cat appears as soon as I have parked my car. No matter where I park. No matter what hour of evening or night. This cat meows loudly at me and hungrily heads right for the food, having watched closely to see where I would place it. Caramel.

But does s/he just wait around in the shed area for me to show up with food? Surely s/he can't be depending solely on my visits.

The meowing, incidentally, tells me that Caramel has HOPE—hope that a person will be doing something good for him or her. Meowing is an expression of hope.

A week ago, I saw another black-and-white cat lying, presumably dead, by the side of the road less than a mile from the building where Silky and her gang "live" or at least hang out. I don't think it was Boots or Snowpatch. Rather than being mostly black with a few well-placed white markings here and there, this large cat was roughly equally black and white, and the colors seemed placed randomly and in a disorderly manner. The cat's body vanished by the next day. It was a sad, disconcerting sight.

A few days ago, the maintenance and safety manager of my workplace, Mr. B. R. King, described to me upgrades being considered to the outside area of the main building (next to the parking lot). The in-ground swimming pool had already been removed, filled in with dirt. A garden might be planted there. Good stuff. Or, this gentleman Mr. King continued, a fancy pavilion might be erected where the pool had been. In that case, the old white storage shed would be torn down. I didn't hear the rest of what he was saying, because *oh no*! That would be the end of the feral cats' home and shelter. Where would they go? This would surely disrupt their lives in a major way. But I very rarely see Silky on the premises anyway, so what do I care?

Saturday, May 1, 2010

Tonight at 10:30 I saw three denizens of the storage shed area. First to appear was, of course, Caramel, meowing and staying close, but not quite close enough to touch. Caramel seemed desperate for food. After a while, Gen-gi headed for the food. Then came Boots or Snowpatch, making a beeline for Cat Haven. It seems that Gen-gi and Boots or Snowpatch defer to Caramel for some reason. I can only assume and hope that Caramel SHARED the food and fresh water with the others tonight. There was plenty of food—two bowlfuls in fact. A bounty.

Two days ago, tipsy from a party at a house just down the road, I placed food at Cat Haven in broad daylight, taking a chance at being spotted! No Caramel in sight. I was hoping that Silky would come by at some point and get her food before Caramel knew it was there. What were the chances of that happening? Slim to none?

Yes, Cat Haven (location A) is now reopen for business. It's where Silky brought her four kittens to escape from some problem she was having with the old white storage shed enclosure area.

Thursday, May 13, 2010

Last night I dreamed I saw Silky lying on her side in a field, eyes open, dead.

Friday, May 14, 2010

Today was a magical day. The children who attend this school, set in this rural agricultural "country" region, held a May Day celebration in honor of the arrival of spring and the bursting forth of new life and color and brightness all around them. There was dancing—both social and ceremonial—and singing, and presenting of flowers.

After a late-afternoon piano lesson, my young student matter-of-factly told me several remarkable accounts of local animals. She attended a class that explores the fields and woods surrounding our building, looking to see what's there. She told of her teacher helping a crow with a broken wing. She also described how, on a "snake hunt" last year, her group encountered four or five baby kittens in a hollow tree with their mother. The mother cat bolted, either up the tree or away from the tree—the child was unclear but clearly excited by the memory. The children could not get at the kittens. They were unreachable. When asked what color the mother cat was, the child replied, "Black." This child thought the baby kittens were adorable, precious.

I wonder what happened to the kittens. How can they survive, thrive? How does the mother cat (and/or the father cat) cope? A hollow tree. Is that any place to have babies? Is it, perhaps, a NICE spot to have babies? Seems to be a safe spot, at any rate. There's so much that goes on that I don't know about and don't see. This sort of thing goes on every day, everywhere on the planet. Amazing.

I stayed late, arranging all of the flowers the children had brought and had placed at the base of the tall, erect, beribboned maypole. I carefully brought inside the huge, green crepe-paper bedecked, foliage-spewing Green Man face that had hung hidden among the branches of a nearby tree, adding that ancient and captivating image to the May Day festivities. S/he is an important and beneficial presence at May Day celebrations. This aged, but still revered, icon more often than not looks like a man, but there are some Green Woman images in existence also. Since we see mostly male depictions throughout history, I will simply refer to it as Green Man.

Because I find myself exploring the relationship between us two-leggeds and all things occurring in Nature, or "the wild," I think it appropriate to weave the Green Man, and related characters, into my story as I progress from here. And Silky, of course, lives outside in the "great out-of-doors" as they say, which is the realm of the Green Man. So since Silky means so much to me, then the environment in which she dwells becomes important for me to consider, especially as to how healthy her environment itself is.

The Green Man is a spirit signifying irrepressible life, thought to be responsible for calling forth vegetation of all kinds. The oldest extant visual representation of the Green Man dates from the first half of the second century. This representation is of a male face formed out of a leaf "mask." It's an astounding work of craftsmanship and inspiration. Similarly, the Green Man is seen in the multitude of carvings of him since then as an organic composite of a human head with vegetation. For this reason, the Green Man has been called the archetype of our oneness with Earth.

The Green Man is seen as the combination of the life force of Nature with the dynamic energy of human life. But the combination is a harmonious one. So that the Green Man, also often assuming the role of Guardian of the Forest, reminds us today that with deforestation at a critical high, there is a universal, communal hope that we can still redeem our relationship with the natural world.

I have seen a sculpted image of a Green Woman face placed at the foot of someone's driveway, there in the grass among some seashells, rocks, and smooth, painted pebbles. She is about ten inches high, painted green in such a way that the design of a wood grain is strongly depicted. Her eyes and her lips are calmly closed—yet she exudes a commanding, majestic, and noble presence. Even with her human facial features sublimely at rest, she expresses something powerful, so I am always impacted, moved, somewhat shaken, by this presence. Interestingly, every time I walk by, her placement has been carefully adjusted, shifted slightly, moved to a different position, often facing in a new direction! In a rather startling manner, the multitude of green leaves surrounding her face seem to be a part of her, growing decorously from her.

Some Green Man authorities have pointed out that the organic composite of human face with vegetation suggests that plant life has intelligence, sensory systems, and an ability to communicate eloquently. Paul Stamets, mycologist of *Fantastic Fungi* fame, declares: "Nature is intelligent. The fact that we lack the language skills to communicate with nature does not impugn the concept that nature's intelligent. It speaks to our inadequacy for communication." He goes on to say, "The task that we face today is to understand the language of nature."[5] But yes, he states that there is definitely an interconnectedness among us. Look to the Leaf Face!

In his book *The Quest for the Green Man*, John Matthews tells us of the Green Man, "Go out into any part of the land at a high point of the year, especially between May and June, and you will feel his presence—in the standing corn and the waving wheat, in the rich greenery of the trees, and in the heavy blossoms that decorate the hedgerows."[6] It is therefore fitting to have May Day celebrations that honor the Green Man at this vibrant, colorful time of year with abundant new vegetation gloriously evident.

Down through the ages of human existence, the Green Man has danced, always present in our psyches, although manifesting in numerous varying forms. For example, due to their similar relationships with woodlands, the Green Man was closely associated with the Greek god Pan, and here it should be noted that Pan, like other nature spirits, appears to be older than the Olympians. Pan was known, first and foremost, as the lord of the wild—unconstrained by the demands of civilization.

In his journal, Henry David Thoreau describes how he finds a "fountain of youth" in the song of the wood thrush. And it's not just that the wood thrush makes him feel young again; it's that the wood thrush is tied, for him, to wild, uncivilized Nature. Thoreau tells us that we need to find the place where the wood thrush forever sings, which is where "eternal morning" is. Where children are, even though only momentarily. Is an eager interest in, even a longing for, the "fountain of youth"

---

[5] *Fantastic Fungi,* directed by Louie Schwartzberg (2019; Moving Art).
[6] John Matthews, *The Quest for the Green Man* (Wheaton, Illinois: Quest Books, 2001).

always lurking somewhere deep in the human psyche? Is there a part of us that regrets having to grow old, to mature, i.e., to leave "wildness," the state of being primitive, behind? Do we love Peter Pan for his ability to refuse "growing up"?

Could there be a connection with Pan in J. M. Barrie's creation of Peter Pan? Or at least an inspiration? I am convinced by Rosalind Ridley's *Peter Pan and the Mind of J. M. Barrie* that there is. Here's what Ridley wrote:

> In the Peter Pan stories, Peter represents a golden age of pre-civilization in both the minds of very young children, before enculturation and education, and in the natural world outside of the influence of humans.[7]

> All children, except one, grow up. They soon know that they will grow up, and the way Wendy knew was this. One day when she was two years old she was playing in a garden, and she plucked a flower and ran with it to her mother. I suppose she must have looked rather delightful, for Mrs. Darling put her hand to her heart and cried, "Oh, why can't you remain like this for ever!" This was all that passed between them on the subject, but henceforth Wendy knew that she must grow up. You always know after you are two. Two is the beginning of the end.[8]

I find myself trying to determine if true wildness (territory apart from, outside of, civilization) still exists somewhere, because this element of "wildness" is important. Thoreau went

---

[7] Rosalind Ridley, *Peter Pan and the Mind of J. M. Barrie: An Exploration of Cognition and Consciousness* (Newcastle upon Tyne, UK: Cambridge Scholars Publishing, 2016).
[8] J.M. Barrie, *Peter and Wendy* (London: Hodder & Stoughton, 1911).

as far as suggesting that "In wildness is the preservation of the world."[9] This quote has stuck with me for a long time, having come across it when I was very young and sensing even then the dire truth in it. Could my quest for *Where the Wild Things Are* (thank you, Maurice Sendak) actually be leading me to the state of childhood, among other territories?

Tinker Bell . . . Yes, Tinker Bell does seem real to young children. And I like the idea of fairies. Well, so did these three esteemed Williams: Shakespeare, Yeats, and Blake.

Thoreau gave the fanciful name of "Fairyland" to the wooded land around Walden Pond in Concord, Massachusetts. This was where he built his famous rustic, ultra-simple cabin—its size was ten feet by fifteen feet, but it did have a cellar. On July 7, 1852, he wrote these words into his Journal: "There is everywhere dew on the cobwebs, little gossamer veils or scarfs as big as your hand, dropped from the fairy shoulders that danced on the grass the past night."[10]

Did the tooth fairy ever visit you during the night and leave you some money for a lost tooth? Maybe you've felt the pull of a Slavic *rusalka* near a river or lake. Have you ever let a genie out of the bottle, as the saying goes? A *saunatonttu* (sauna elf), according to Finnish folklore, exists under sauna benches close to the floor, therefore swearing and passing gas are no-nos in saunas because we wouldn't want to upset the sauna elf. Try hard not to upset a djinn either.

There are so many notions about fairies and elves over the course of so many centuries and from so many cultures. It's a testament to our huge and enduring collective imagination. And no

---

[9] Henry David Thoreau, "Walking," Atlantic, 1862, https://www.theatlantic.com/magazine/archive/1862/06/walking/304674/.
[10] Eliot Porter, "In Wildness Is the Preservation of the World," Sierra Club, San Francisco, 1962.

one takes them more seriously than children. During the play and the movie, Peter Pan implores the children to clap their hands if they believe in fairies in order to keep Tinker Bell alive. And what happens, you may ask, if no one claps during this scene? Well, Tinker Bell will die. But don't worry. They always clap.

Do you have the essence of the fairy tale within you? Wendy Froud, famous for being a sculptor and puppet maker in Muppets creator Jim Henson's Creature Shop, said this: "Faeries are spirits of nature. They embody the wild, mysterious and spiritual forces to be found in nature, and help us to reconnect with wonder and mystery inside our own souls."[11] (This quote would also apply to "fairies.")

Check out Shakespeare's *A Midsummer Night's Dream*: Oberon and Titania may be flimsy fairies, King and Queen though they are, but they are powerful representations of certain strong elements of our human personas and souls.

Pan's dynamism continues today. In Washington, DC, there is a well-known and much-loved bronze sculpture of Pan—looking to me like a young faun, a boyish satyr, or, since he is playing a pipe, one of many "little Pans" venerated in ancient Greece. Having existed in several different locations in DC since the 1920s, it has now come to rest in the Bishop's Garden, designed by its creators to be a "garden for the ages," at the Washington National Cathedral. This magical, compelling sculpture was made by Edith Parsons. It now sits at the entrance to the secluded gazebo in the Garden, which is called "Shadow House." It has been installed there on a base inscribed by the cathedral's own stone carvers in dedication to the memory of Washington National Cathedral stained glass artist Rowan LeCompte.

---

[11] I don't recall where I read the Wendy Froud quote, only that Wendy Froud said it.

I find this juxtaposition of Pan with LeCompte fascinating. How is a pagan deity featured with such honor at a Christian place of worship? LeCompte created over forty stained glass windows in the great building, including the large West Rose ("Creation") window, often used as a symbol for this Cathedral.

In his poem "In Just-Spring," E. E. Cummings portrays an image of a goat-footed balloon man with a far-reaching, enticing whistle. Surely this goat-footed character with his irrepressible whistling is a manifestation of Pan. I feel that it is somehow significant that Cummings has his Pan appear at that very special time of year, "in just-spring."

So, we need to go to Peter Pan Park in London, where there is a bronze statue by Sir George Frampton that depicts our hero surrounded by adulating, worshipful fairies, squirrels, mice and bunnies. We need to have a wild, childlike snowball fight around Peter Pan's statue while he plays his long, curved pipes (which are ever so suggestive of panpipes!).

Friday, May 14, 2010 (continued)

At 7:30 p.m., I finally headed for my car, by this time the last one in the parking lot. As I started the motor purring, I glanced straight ahead out of the windshield before I would then turn my head to check behind me in order to back out of the parking space. Right in front of me, half hidden in early lily foliage—there. Yes, unmistakable. The black form of the head and upper body of a very special black cat, silhouetted against the white painted cinderblock wall, staring at me, on high alert.

I slowly emerged from my car and approached her, coaxing, "Silkeee . . . hey baby . . ." I got close enough to check the eye color and chest marking, confirming that it was indeed Silky, before she ducked to hide behind the lily leaf blades.

I was struck by the wonderful juxtaposition of my Green Man/Pan/Peter Pan ruminations and the sudden, unexpected appearance of Silky. I felt that there was something significant in that. Surely the cosmos intended for me to make an important connection between these dearly cherished subjects. Surely there is some interplay among them. Is feral Silky herself a territory of wildness, where wildness can still be found in our highly civilized world? And does Silky take sustenance and joy from her dance with the Green Man?

Oh, love—my life whole again! I told her to wait. "Please don't go away. I have something." (Probably, hopefully, needless things to say to Silky.) I drove home, got cat food and fresh water, and drove back to the parking lot. She was now sitting outside the storage shed and trash area enclosure, jet black, a beautiful shape against the white-painted wooden structure. I called to her and placed her paper bowls nearby. She came to the food almost immediately and fell to. As I watched her approach, I could see that she was thin—too thin? She ate steadily; she was very hungry. I guess that's why she found me. And right out in the open.

I got a chance to hear her voice too. While she was sitting bolt upright near the lilies, she started to meow as I came close to her. She made a delicate, small, high, thin, clear sound, barely opening her mouth. Plaintive sounding. I hadn't been providing food for quite some time, having been too busy with other things. Later, as I prepared to go home, leaving Silky with her food and fresh water, I saw Caramel. Silky beat you to it tonight, eh Caramel? S/he was sitting—on high alert—at a distance from Silky's food bowls, at Cat Haven, staring at me pointedly. Well, only one thing to do. See to Caramel as well. And Caramel received quite a feast.

I adjusted the position of the Kosta Boda bowls (Again, who purchases Kosta Boda crystal for an animal to use?)

because I had noticed that the bowls were in a position to be easily spotted. It could not surprise me if the men in charge of maintenance are "on" to me. They (particularly Mr. B. R. King, a man of power as the influential head of property maintenance) are against encouraging the feral cats by feeding them. I will be reprimanded if they figure out that I am the culprit. I don't know if they would issue an ultimatum, but perhaps, rather ridiculously, they would. They don't think it's a healthy situation to have feral cats around; they believe these shy, quiet creatures will attack us any chance they get, howling and screaming, giving us cat scratch fever or some other awful ailment.

But do they realize that I feed the cats only occasionally, not giving them nearly enough on which to survive, and that in doing so, I am only searching for Silky? I feel I'm on an important quest, but it's not yet clear to me exactly what I'm searching for. But it involves Silky; I know that much.

Tonight (still May 14), I went back to the parking lot to get rid of the "evidence" (meaning the two paper bowls Silky had used), but there was, unexpectedly, a sheriff in a police car sitting at the exact spot where Silky had eaten her food. I quickly waved with forced politeness, turned around, and immediately drove away. Wonder what HE thought.

I wondered why Caramel had let Silky have all of the first food serving in peace. Caramel sat quietly at Cat Haven, watching Silky eat. This was unusual behavior for Caramel.

*　*　*

Maybe Silky represents "insight" to me—flashing insight. Insight occurs just as Silky's appearances occur to me, suddenly, like a bright flash—exciting, galvanizing, fully capturing my attention, satisfying. And yes, I'm searching for insight . . . constantly.

Maybe Silky represents "divine guidance." How about that? It's certainly something worthy of seeking, of going on a quest for. Pointers from another world, another realm, a higher realm. And do we recognize it when we come across it? Do we know it for sure when we see it, especially in the darkness? It would need to be something that stands apart from the common, everyday, ordinary, human (and therefore flawed, disappointing) guideposts that we find ourselves following. Could Silky be a metaphor for divine guidance? Such a thing would certainly warrant heartfelt searching, prayers, yearning, and the hope that "never stops at all," being Emily Dickinson's "thing with feathers that perches in the soul."

* * *

Maybe what Silky represents is in her name. I must have chosen that name for a (subconscious) reason. It must be a metaphor for something elusive but grand. Maybe in this life I seek what the word "silky" suggests—smoothness, refinement, luster, easy going along life's path, luxury.

Monday, May 24, 2010

I pulled into the parking lot for some work I needed to get done in the building after hours. (Not. I just wanted to greet my cat.) Soon thereafter, Caramel (S/he heard my car!) appeared at the far end of the lot, at the shed, waiting expectantly, watching me, meowing. I eventually (waiting for Silky to show up) found a spot in the front garden in which to place some cat food and water in paper bowls. Cat Haven had been sprayed earlier with some sort of (maybe toxic) weed killer, so I planned to abandon that spot for a while and wouldn't be using those "permanent" glass bowls until I'd washed them.

Caramel was at the paper bowls in two shakes of a lamb's tail, preparing to pounce on the food. I went inside and fiddled around for a while, then wandered out again and moved my car to a spot right out in front of the building so that I could collect quickly and easily the evidence of the used paper bowls. I thought the feeding location was out of sight, at least of the cleaning folks who had observed me before, in another part of this garden, doing cat feeding business. I fear they think I'm crazy.

I stepped into the garden to collect the paper bowls, and behold, a latecomer had arrived to find them—empty, thanks to Caramel's assertive and tenacious domination of the cat-feeding scene. The latecomer was Silky, hungry and searching. (Searching For Nancy?) I spoke to her soothingly and promisingly and watched her closely, thrilled with the close encounter. I picked up the bowl to refill it with food for Silky, thinking it was something I could easily do to care for my cat and strengthen our connection. As I turned around to get more food, still wheedling and mewing energetically, I was startled to see a good friend of mine standing there, right in front of me! I guess he had spotted me from the main road (a rural road with very little traffic where everything nearby stands out and is noticed). He worked at the building also—a colleague. He asked what in the world was I doing—picking flowers? "Yes. Yes, of course," I said, trying to make the paper bowl in my hand as inconspicuous as possible. I didn't want it to be known that I was feeding feral cats on school property. I continued to fear repercussions from doing something that was ostensibly against school policy.

He got into his truck and pulled it forward to the main entrance of the building, stopped, and got out. I thought of the first few lines of a poem by Robert Frost:

When a friend calls to me from the road
And slows his horse to a meaning walk,
I don't stand still and look around
On all the hills I haven't hoed,
And shout from where I am, What is it?
No, not as there is a time to talk.[12]

I climbed into my car immediately, forced to ignore Silky and her quest for food. I then slowly and casually advanced toward his truck. We were friends, so obviously a friendly conversation must now take place. I couldn't just drive past him, heading for home, which I knew was where I now had to head, no muss, no fuss, no more weird hanging around, wandering in the garden at the front of the building, where there were actually no flowers. I drove reluctantly toward him, good friend though he was.

We exchanged friendly chitchat, mostly consisting of me wildly admiring the gardens on the building's premises and explaining how I was not above cutting a few of the pretty flowers to bring home or to cheer up a sick person. Musing, and with but a faint smile, he regarded me somewhat skeptically. If he had another question as to why I was milling around, bumbling about among the shrubbery and ornamental trees, cooing loudly and coaxingly in a high-pitched voice, he kept it to himself. Then, after smiling broadly and waving warmly at

---

12 Excerpt from "A Time to Talk" by Robert Frost.

my friend, I had to completely turn my back on Silky, and get out of there, drive home with no further ado.

Mission not accomplished. Mission approaching successful completion, then abruptly aborted. I felt so agitated—for Silky's sake. I kept seeing her face staring me down, hoping, counting on me, and then I had to ignore and deny her. I couldn't come through for her, even though we'd had a close and intimate encounter, the very thing I want to encourage. I wished I hadn't actually seen her so close and then spoken to her because then I had to follow it up with NOTHING.

It created such a feeling of angst within me. But why? I do feel that an important aspect of my journey, my quest, involves taking care of Silky, nourishing Silky. She must be a metaphor for something, although I'm not yet sure what.

And Caramel scores again.

And now I would have to go back late at night, when I could be sure no one would be around to see me, to retrieve the paper water bowl so the maintenance men wouldn't see it first thing in the morning and become suspicious. Although maybe they would assume it was random trash from a place where, after all, CHILDREN congregate every day.

So I made the short trip back to my workplace from home much later, in order to retrieve the paper water bowl. Guess what I saw come running across the lot toward me as I got out of my car. Caramel. Of course. Does s/he ever go out to hunt? S/he's the only one who always seems to be there. Maybe I'm not doing Caramel any favors by providing food; perhaps it could be to Caramel's detriment in the end?

Wednesday, May 26, 2010

Today while the children who spend their days at the building where I work were outside playing, one came to me and gave me a Silly Band in the shape of an electric guitar. It was one of many in her extensive collection of Silly Bandz—she knows I love music.

Later, a crowd of children stood around me while I showed off my new Silly Band. One little boy stepped forward and begged to have it, offering a Silly Band from HIS extensive collection as a trade. I was reluctant to give up the guitar, which everyone knew was fabulous, but I wanted to make him happy, so I finally agreed to trade. It did indeed please him greatly to be the new owner of the lime-green electric guitar Silly Band. What he tossed to me in exchange was . . . a cat!

Did he know how much a cat would mean to me, especially coming from him? Maybe, maybe not. His mother is Mrs. Vet, the very veterinarian who had spayed Silky for me, tested her blood to make sure she's healthy, and inoculated her against feline diseases. His mother had collected Silky's four kittens and taken them into her home to domesticate them and take care of them, with an eye to eventually placing them into good homes and living situations.

When I captured Silky and brought her to their house for medical treatment, I had observed this very boy (something of a wild thing himself) in a small, special room with the four tiny kittens crawling all over him. He was content, calm, and highly focused, learning from his vet mother how to go about "gentling" these feral creatures. As I watched this boy now, I recalled how impressive his expertise was in handling the kittens. He had looked so darling and sweet and was so very caring of his wild little charges. And he had only been in first grade, young Zackitty Vet.

Friday, May 28, 2010

Today, while driving home, I spied a deceased cat on top of a stucco wall right next to the road, several miles from my home and workplace. I turned around and drove back for a second look—yes, deceased, not sleeping. The body was black with tall white boots. And a feral cat, I guess. Would a cat owner have allowed his/her dead cat to lie there like that?

I can't think of what to name this cat. Boots and Snow-patch are good, but those names are already taken, of course. Not that that matters, I suppose. Anyway, does one name a cat already dead? John or Jane Doe is obviously not suitable. John Cat or Jane Cat? Tom Paw might be good, but can that name be used if it's a female cat? Maybe this cat already has a name.

Did s/he die there in that spot on top of the narrow cement wall? Seems odd. Did someone place Jane or John Paw there? The scene raised questions. It was a jarring sight right next to the little road; one could see the details . . . My husband across the river has remarked that death is "just a cat's whisker away." Is he right? Are we so very close to death even as we function normally and go about the process of living, going about our daily business? And how did Jane or John Paw die? Maybe a more important question is: Does a cat have nine lives? And anyway, how does that work?

Saturday, May 29, 2010

Two cats enjoyed the food and water I provided this evening, Gentle Giant and Caramel. A cousin of mine, Marya

Hahldatter, was staying with me for the weekend, and she gladly came along and sat with me to watch the cats at their meal. Caramel had been on the lookout for me in a prominent position at the head of the parking lot where the driveway rises up a small hill and from where s/he could survey the main road on which the building is located—in other words, detect my approach.

As Caramel started eating, Gen-gi appeared out of the shadows and casually joined in, but as usual never showed the ravenous intensity of Caramel. Marya and I observed contrasting behaviors between the two cats. Gen-gi basically reclined in the parking lot, sphinxlike, after eating—lying low, calm and still, but ever listening for interesting sounds. Gen-gi is a large cat with a big bushy tail and a coat of dull, dusky black. Caramel did some dainty grooming after s/he ate and sat up with tail curled around body. S/he has regular, "perfect" patterned markings of attractive stripes on a glossy, beigey-orange coat. S/he has a slender tail.

I remembered last summer when Caramel first appeared (to me) on the scene. S/he was a kitten. The other cats had treated Caramel roughly and aggressively and, it would seem, with some hostility. I had been shocked to watch this. However, it could be that I'd misinterpreted the actions of the other cats; maybe it's part of feral cat training, preparation for the tough, harsh, hardscrabble existence they face?

Where had Caramel come from? S/he didn't look at all like, or behave very much like, the other cats. One thing, Caramel always seems very hungry and desperately dependent on the occasional food I supply of an evening or sometimes late at night.

Sunday, May 30, 2010

This morning, as Marya and I drove through the tiny town not far from the building where I work and where the feral cat gang in this story hangs out, we spotted Caramel outside one of the houses. This was surprising to me. I couldn't imagine any of the feral gang wandering openly about the town during broad daylight. But the little town seemed to be Caramel's stomping grounds, as was the outlying institution where I had been feeding this attractive and well-groomed animal. Marya wondered if Caramel could be someone's outdoor cat. Again, where had Caramel come FROM when, as a kitten, s/he appeared on the scene last summer in the parking lot of the building where I work? Born there? Where WAS Caramel born, and what cats, and where, are Caramel's mother and father, brothers and sisters?

Monday, June 7, 2010

Last night as I headed home, I stopped at the nearby building where I work. It was 11:00. I pulled into a space in the parking lot and saw, sitting right in front of me on a pile of mulch, Caramel. Caramel does not follow the rule of staying HIDDEN, which all of the other feral cats in the gang do. And Caramel does not stay SILENT either, like the other cats on the scene do, with the noteworthy exception of when Silky recently (May 14) spoke directly to me, taking me by surprise by sharing with me the sound of her voice.

Anyway, tonight Caramel was joined by Gen-gi and Boots or Snowpatch for the meal. I thought I saw Silky right behind my car at one point, but I couldn't be sure because this cat dashed away, to my dismay and frustration. Of all the feral cats, Silky seems the most terrified around me.

Sunday, June 13, 2010

Last night at 11:00, Caramel and Gen-gi showed up for some food shortly after I arrived. They shared the food in the little paper bowl by butting heads together gently, now and then shoving a head into full control of the bowl. Caramel looked very thin. It pains me to see an animal going hungry, getting thinner and thinner, skinnier than a toothpick with termites. We can't have that, can we? Caramel kept his/her tail straight up into the air the entire time. I wonder what that signifies. Gen-gi enjoyed some fresh water. Caramel eschewed the water.

I don't use Cat Haven these days.

Tuesday, June 15, 2010

10:30 p.m.
Caramel and Gen-gi.

Friday, June 18, 2010

9:45 p.m.
Caramel.

Tuesday, June 29, 2010

It had been a week or so since my last visit to the cats with food and water. After choir practice, I stopped by the parking lot at work on my way home. It was 8:30, a lovely summer evening. Caramel appeared shortly, and I provided the famished cat with a bowl of canned cat food and a bowl of water. S/he went through the one bowlful of food, then a second bowlful, this one of dry food. This eager beaver polished off TWO bowls with no monkeying around.

I sat in my car and observed the scene. I gazed in all directions around me, scanning the rural, cleared but only slightly developed land, searching for a special, beloved black cat. Yes, I was searching for Silky, absolutely.

There was no reason to think I would see Silky this evening, or at any other time, really—Silky sightings are as scarce as hens' teeth. However, I eventually spotted a smallish black form stalking stealthily and warily along a distant fence with hedges and tall grass growing beside it. Could it be? This jet-black creature was in front of me, but at some distance (a field) away. I called, "Silky, Silkeeee, come on, Silky, come on, Silky!" The animal obviously heard my voice and recognized it as coming from someone of interest, someone who had provided food before—knew it as a voice that came from ME. My voice drew the creature in. So yes, it was a smallish black cat, and I soon recognized the striking figure and bright, piercing eyes! The fact that Silky came to me when I called her was a huge turning point in my connection with her!

I produced a third bowl of food and encouraged Silky toward it and the insatiable Caramel away from it. Silky bolted to my car and lurked there, then came toward the food I offered. And though Caramel approached Silky and her food a few times, s/he never got too close; Caramel seemed respectful of her. Silky took a few sips of water, ate most of the food, and then immediately took off, removing herself to a distant little tree near an intersection of two small roads at a far corner of the property. After sitting under the tree for a while, she crossed over the intersection, catty-corner, into a woodsy area. Gone.

Meanwhile, Caramel, never one to demur, polished off the remains of Silky's bowl of food. Caramel is one hungry cat. Why is s/he so hungry all the time? Not like the other cats in the gang. Caramel hangs around, also. Again, unlike the others.

Thursday, July 1, 2010

I drove to the parking lot of my workplace at 8:15 p.m. Caramel was reclining alertly at the corner of the storage shed. Why do cats like to be at corners of buildings? Waiting there for something, waiting to surprise? Caramel fixated on me and waited expectantly for the food and water bowls. S/he fell to and enjoyed a complete can of food.

Another cat lurked inside the nearby trash enclosure attached to the side of the storage shed but did not emerge to approach the food. It looked like Gen-gi to me, so I filled another bowl with dry food and set it at one of the openings the cats use to enter and exit the trash enclosure area. These openings were created where a few of the wooden slats of the fence had broken off at the bottom. Sure enough, Gen-gi emerged and started eating the new bowlful, soon to be joined by none other than Silky! Gasp, double take. Whoa, Nelly! Really? I didn't see THAT coming. Literally. Yes, Silky materialized out of thin air to take her place at the food bowl. I refilled the first bowl with dry food and lured the tense, jumpy Silky toward it. She ate most of it, then had some water— quite a bit, actually.

At one point, Caramel, who thinks s/he is entitled to ALL food bowls, approached Silky, and a hissing match ensued, which Silky won. Caramel backed off.

When Silky was finished with her food, leaving a small amount for Caramel to polish off, she headed for a tree near the parking lot to sit and take the evening air and bathe herself.

Later, when she saw me preparing to leave, she came back and sat at the edge of the parking lot to watch.

I guess I'm training Silky not to be afraid that I will trap her in a cage and take her to someone's garage, then to be given treatment which might include grabbing, poking, and shots. And have I just succeeded in adding Silky to the feral cat gang at my workplace, who look to be fed by me on a semi-regular basis? If so, Maintenance and Administration won't be pleased. "The cats are not to be encouraged" is their attitude.

At one point during tonight's red-letter feeding event, Boots or Snowpatch arrived at a far end of the parking lot, quietly observed the goings-on from afar, and then just as quietly left the scene. The silent, calm arrival and departure of Boots or Snowpatch reminded me of Carl Sandburg's "Fog." Sandburg suggests that the movement of fog is as if "on little cat feet." And then, continuing the comparison, the poet says that after sitting "on silent haunches" looking over the area, the fog simply moves on.

Sunday, August 15, 2010

It was announced to me today via snail mail, perhaps in consideration of those of us who have vacated the campus for the summer, that a brand-new (red) storage shed has been built, and that a new garbage dumpster stall will soon be built next to it, all of this allowing for the imminent tearing-down of the "ugly eyesore" of the current old white storage shed/dumpster stall. The plan is to improve sightlines to an area where the young human inhabitants of the building gather every day for exercise, fresh air, and free play.

But the doomed structure is home to the feral cats, a place providing shelter, a hiding spot, warmth in the winter, safety, and the occasional food scrap or two, either from people who see them or from the garbage dumpsters, and near to useful things such as bird baths from which to get fresh rain-water. What will happen to the cats?

But then I suppose a feral cat can't be anything if not resourceful and adaptable, so why worry? But then again, their familiar environment must mean something to them, must have some importance for them. The new red storage shed, by the way, is not hospitable to wild animals; all along the bottom of the structure, a barrier was put into place, effectively block-ing all access to the area underneath. No animal could ever gain entry into or under this stronghold.

Maybe now would be a good time to stop paying atten-tion to the local feral cats—the "Ferals" as my husband across the river refers to them, as if they are some sort of family group. He has a cat named Kitty, and he often threatens to exile her to live with "the Ferals" if she doesn't shape up and behave herself. "How would you like to go and live with the FERALS??"

It grows harder and harder for me to find the energy and time to feed and observe the cats. Plus, I'm becoming paranoid about it. I feel people could be catching on to what I'm doing, and it's not exactly sanctioned by the powers that be in the institution where the cats live (and HAVE LIVED for quite some time, I might add). At the very least, I'm worried that the proprietors, and neighbors, of my rented farm-caretaker's house wonder what the heck I'm up to, leaving my house late at night, headlights blazing, after everything is closed up tight for the night, and then returning half an hour or an hour later. I know I would wonder about a tenant exhibiting such an odd behavior pattern.

I also wonder if perhaps I'm not helping the ferals in the end. They need to be capable hunters and skilled foragers, either finding enough food and water locally and of their own devices, or else moving on—or even dying off if Nature wants it that way. I don't know, really, what I'm saying here. I just have vague doubts about what I'm doing with these ferals. Maybe now, with their home structure, the old storage shed, being torn down, I should help effect a change in where these cats dwell. Maybe now I should pull away from them completely and concentrate on other things, like my very real (and quite demanding) job, and go back to treating my workplace like a workplace rather than a haven for wild animals.

Friday, August 27, 2010

To keep the campus free of permanently placed, and noticeable, bowls sitting around here and there, I've used paper bowls these days, set at the sides of the old shed next to the trash dumpster area. I place them next to the wall so they don't slide around while the poor cats are trying to eat, for sometimes parts of the black parking lot pavement surface are as slick as owl grease. If it's a weekend evening, I can leave the bowls out and stop by the next day to make them disappear. If it's a weeknight, I stay until the cats (Caramel) finish the food, and then I clear the bowls away so there's no chance of arousing suspicion early the next morning when Maintenance and other staff arrive on the scene.

Yes, lately it's only been Caramel, sometimes with Gen-gi, eating my cat food. I worry especially about Caramel. I wonder if Caramel has been declawed—domesticated, then abandoned from the home s/he'd had, dropped off by the side of the road, or went away from it for some other reason (accidentally let out), and then perhaps got lost or left behind, left to make do somehow in the great out-of-doors. But don't I remember Caramel as a kitten at the storage shed?

Generally speaking, am I really doing these cats any favors? Have I made them dependent on me and my feedings, removing from them their will and motivation and determination—yes, their NEED—to constantly perfect their hunting and foraging skills? By giving them handouts, am I encouraging complacency and discouraging the honing of hunting, scrounging, and fishing—skills a desperately hungry cat would otherwise be honing?

And I know of at least two people who work at the building where the feral cats hang out who believe that feeding them is a no-no, I suppose because feeding them encourages their presence. It's only two, but they happen to be influential people. Quite a while ago, the one of them who is in charge of the maintenance crew, Mr. King, had sent a series of grim, stern emails to all of us who work at the campus, inveighing against feeding "the cats," and demanding to know who was doing it. I had been surprised and bemused by these emails, wondering what cats he was talking about and which one of us was taking the trouble to feed them. *There are cats?* I said to myself, and, *Who is the villain who is trying to feed them?* This was long before I encountered Silky face-to-face in the garden with her kittens. The other is of course our Mr. Bark, devoted maintenance man and landscape specialist.

No doubt these men have righteous reasons for their negative attitudes toward the feral cats and for their disapproval of their presence on the campus. The men are motivated by a desire to protect, and keep healthy, the community of people that frequent the buildings and their surrounding property. They wish to ensure our welfare and the sound and attractive condition of everything on the campus. We should keep in mind that these men have our best interests at heart. I know they take very seriously the safety of the children who go in and out of the buildings of the campus all day long and sometimes at night.

However. Having said all of that, I really must disparage Mr. Bark's oft-expressed belief that these cats will attack the children who are in and out of the building during the day; I can't imagine such a thing happening. And the fact that he suggested glue-trapping these cats, referring in that conversation specifically to Silky, taxes my amenability even more, especially since he actually thought the idea was amusing.

Tonight, after grocery shopping, I stopped by the parking lot with a newly purchased can of wet food, a new bag of dry food, and some water bottles. The first cat I saw was unfamiliar to me in behavior and coloring. Not seeming "car conscious" at all, this one didn't get out of the path of my car until the very last minute. FINALLY realizing a car was steadily bearing down right behind, this cat headed for a grassy area next to the pavement. The cat was black with a small, but very clear, pronounced white bib and short white boots. The cat disappeared and didn't seem to expect that I would soon be serving food.

Meanwhile, laying low but on high alert in another grassy area close by, was the ever-ready Caramel, watching me like a hawk. I set out a bowl of wet food and a bowl of water at the dumpster enclosure. Caramel was there immediately.

But in the darkness, my eyes soon discerned a tiny creature joining Caramel at the food bowl. This was a much smaller animal than I was used to seeing. I approached close enough to determine that it was a kitten! Tawny orange in color, with little stripes, it was a tiny Caramel! The kitten was very afraid of me and pranced and jumped quickly into the dumpster enclosure whenever I came close.

While I observed from a distance back at my car, I soon detected another small form, this one black, that bolted into the dumpster enclosure whenever I approached. When the tiny black shape stayed outside long enough for me to get a good look, I realized it was a new black kitten!

Two kittens were now part of the small gang with the old storage shed as their home. I set out another bowl of dry food near where the black kitten had emerged, and the kitten came out and began to eat. Crunch, crunch, crunch! Also, Grrrrrr! These cats growled softly but threateningly while they ate. Soon, a bigger black cat joined the black kitten, but it was too dark to figure out the identity of the bigger cat; I couldn't see the markings.

Then the big black cat drove the black kitten away from the food bowl by clawing at the little creature. But as I drove away, they were eating together again at that same bowl. Caramel was actually more willing to share, moving over so that the little Caramel could have equal time at their shared bowl.

Kittens. Must be siblings. How long? When? Which cats? Caramel? What will become of them? What . . . Where . . . How . . . So many questions. Will the family group stay together? It's hard to fathom and describe how I felt about this new development. I was fascinated, yes. Charmed and enchanted, check. Mesmerized, yes. I was also worried, fearful, dismayed, yes, I was. But overall, I felt love—for all of them.

So would now be a good time, after all, to stop thinking of the ferals, stop providing food and fresh water, even going so far as to get them neutered and inoculated as I'd done for Silky? Now? At this particular time? Would this be a good time to start ignoring these cats?

How can I? Even if now WOULD be the right time to stop feeding these cats, I don't think I can give up searching for Silky, which involves feeding these cats, I believe. I'm so lucky to have made the acquaintance of Silky—to have connected with this marvelous animal. Yes, I must look for more encounters, evoke her somehow. Why does she behave the way she does? I would like to nurture her . . . OR is it her very wildness that appeals to me?

But Silky will probably find ME, rather than the other way around. She has proved to be good at that; I give HER something in addition to her giving me something. Silky has a history with me at this building. She'll always have that and carry it with her, ambivalent as she might be about a part of that history. Perhaps I've done all I can, and should do, for Silky. But has Silky finished with me? Has she finished giving to me all that SHE can, or all that I need from her?

* * *

People have said over the years, in different ways, that it's not the destination that is so important, but rather the journey.

Arthur Ashe: "Success is a journey, not a destination. The doing: often more important than the outcome."

Ursula K. Le Guin: "It is good to have an end to journey toward; but it is the journey that matters, in the end."

Pattie Gonia (Life On Purpose movement): "The finish line is for the ego. The journey is for the soul."

Mahatma Gandhi: "The path is the goal."

Also to be considered here, Jesus Christ stated, "I am the way."[13] According to the book of John in the Bible, during the Last Supper, Jesus told His disciples that He would soon be leaving, going to a place where eventually the disciples would meet Him. Thomas and the other disciples were anxiously concerned, and Thomas said, "Lord, we do not know where you are going; how can we know the way?"[14] The amazing reply was that Jesus IS the way!

This process of searching for Silky is taking such a long time. It feels as if I'm on a journey now. But I don't know where I'm aiming to go! Nevertheless, I feel a strong need to continue on. Where will all of this lead? To what?

This Buddhist teaching "The path is the goal" is certainly relevant. Here is an excerpt from a discussion of this teaching, found in Pema Chödrön's *When Things Fall Apart*:

> This is a very encouraging teaching, because it says that the source of wisdom is whatever is going to happen to us today. The source of wisdom is whatever is happening to us right at this very instant.[15]

---

[13] From John 14:6, "I am the way and the truth and the life. No one comes to the Father except through me." (New International Version).

[14] John 14:5 (New International Version).

[15] Pema Chödrön, *When Things Fall Apart: Heart Advice for Difficult Times* (Washington, DC: National Geographic Books, 2007).

And here's another excerpt from the same book:

> This path has one very distinct characteristic: it is
> not pre-fabricated. It doesn't already exist. The
> path that we're talking about is the moment-by-
> moment evolution of our experience, the moment-
> by-moment evolution of the world of phenomena,
> the moment-by-moment evolution of our thoughts
> and our emotions.[16]

"The path is the goal." Jean-Paul Sartre said that there are two ways to go to the gas chamber: free or not free. So all things, not just some things, are workable, according to Buddhist teaching—even something as appalling as a doomed walk to the gas chamber. Sartre says that the journey TO the gas chamber is the most important thing, rather than the gas chamber experience itself; we can work that journey in such a way as to be free rather than enslaved.

Regarding the many hours I spend in the school parking lot—basically just hanging around, placing catfood here and there, watching, waiting quietly—according to what I learn from Buddhist tradition, these activities hold great importance! They comprise the path, the journey, the quest, the process. So I will continue my search. And I believe that FINDING Silky, which is my ostensible goal anyway, actually represents finding something far more significant and profound. I feel sure that the search for this mysterious something is of great consequence.

---

[16] Ibid.

Searching For Lambs

English

1. As I went out— one May morn-ing, One May morn-ing— be-time, I met a maid— from— home had strayed— Just as the sun— did shine.

2. What makes you rise so soon, my dear,
   Your journey to pursue?
   Your pretty little feet they tread so sweet,
   Strike off the morning dew.

3. I'm going to feed my father's flock,
   His young and tender lambs,
   That over hills and over dales
   Lie waiting for their dams.

4. O stay! O stay! you handsome maid,
   And rest a moment here,
   For there is none but you alone,
   That I do love so dear.

5. How gloriously the sun doth shine,
   How pleasant is the air,
   I'd rather rest on a true love's breast
   Than any other where.

6. For I am thine, and thou art mine;
   No man shall uncomfort thee;
   We'll join our hands in wedded bands
   And married we will be.

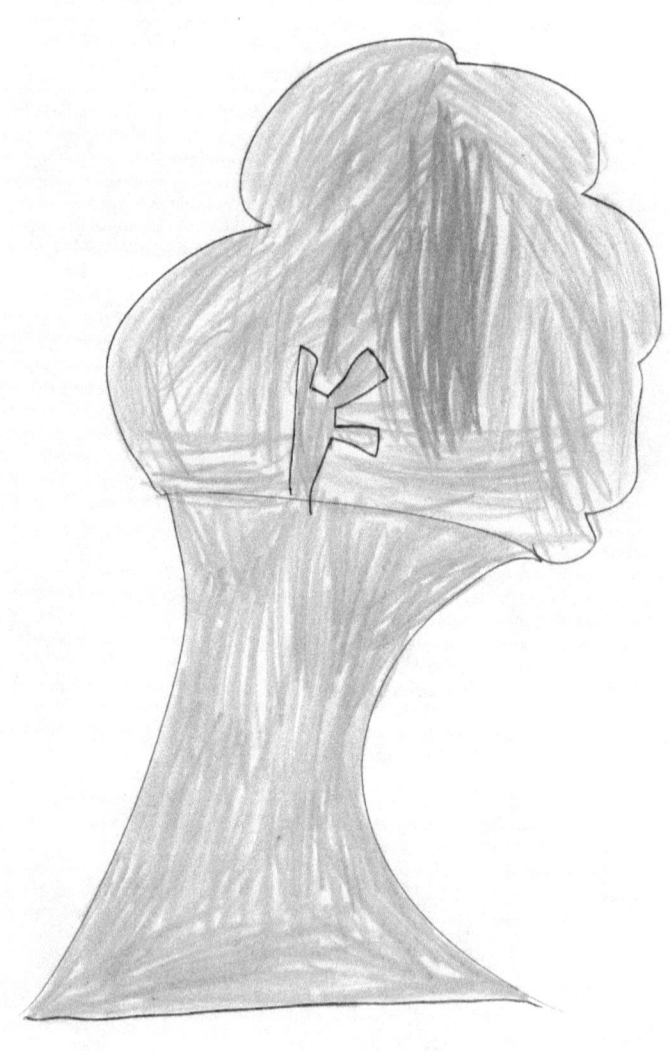

Thursday, September 2, 2010

I had a conversation today with a staff member called Ms. B. D. Driver. (Ms. Driver, by the way, was the "guilty" party of Mr. King's aforementioned reproachful emailed complaints regarding the cat feeding that he noticed occurring in the school parking lot, pre2009.)

Here is what she told me:

- Silky birthed her four kittens underneath the old white storage shed. All was well until something happened to make her move her brood to the front garden. Driver wondered if it might have been that she was being (purposely?) blocked from getting under the shed to her kittens, which Silky would surely have found frustrating, to say the least. I had heard from another source that at about that time, rat poison had been applied under that shed, I guess to kill snakes that were thought to be living there. I wouldn't think Silky would find this acceptable in a place to raise kittens either. It is unknown what actually happened to prompt Silky to go to the trouble of moving her kittens away from the shed (and to Cat Haven), but she certainly did a good job of it. She kept them with her, safe, and all together.

- The maintenance crew fears cat-scratch fever from the feral cats. And I had gathered previously that another worry of the maintenance men is that the feral cats will attract "other outdoor creatures." I wondered about this possibility. Perhaps other animals would be attracted to the feral cats in order to stalk, attack, or prey upon them? Ooooooh, the kittens . . . On the other hand, maybe the cats would succeed in CLEARING the campus of "other outdoor creatures"?

- Families sometimes take these cats to own—it's a fact.

- A previous maintenance man for our campus, talented local landscaper Mr. Jeffrey Pat D. Drumman, loves the ferals.

- Right at this time, Ms. Driver and one of the children who visit the building every day have been feeding milk to the new kittens and trying to "tame" them so that they could be "taken into a home."

- Silky was, herself, a kitten born under the old white storage shed. Silky has a brother who has been lost. Ms. Driver took this brother to live with her, and she named him Kitten. He is solid black. This is how he got lost: Driver lent him to a friend of hers for the purpose of catching mice. Driver's friend left a door open at the house, and Kitten got out and ran away. Driver has put up a sign in their area that says something like "Please pray for Kitten—he is lost and frightened." Driver misses her cat. She is worried about him and desperately wants him back.

I asked Driver why she thought Kitten might be frightened. "You can't move cats," she answered. "They are homebound." She said she has found out that, unlike dogs, cats want and need to be in a familiar environment; they want to be where they know they're safe . . . "They're territorial," she continued, and she pointed out that it's one of the reasons for the term "scaredy cat."

*　*　*

Mr. Drumman's favorite owl is the barn owl. This fact has nothing to do with the story I'm telling.

* * *

Saturday, September 11, 2010

When I arrived at the parking lot at 9:30 p.m., a kitten or two were busy exploring the area around their home, the old storage shed. A larger black cat, with a small, but very clear, pronounced white bib resembling bright starlight, materialized and looked for food from me, and THREE kittens gathered around this larger cat—two black, and a striped caramel-colored one! When I approached with the bowls of food and water, the kittens dove under the shed. Pretty soon, they emerged and ate their food. The large black cat with sparkling white bib, henceforth referred to as Starlight, did not eat much food, while I was observing anyway, but rather let the kittens indulge themselves. Starlight sat close by, watching the kittens eat and also alertly keeping an eye on the surrounding area. Caramel was not there, not present at the scene!

A surely traumatic event for the ferals is fast approaching. It has been announced that their old weathered white shed will be torn down this coming Saturday, September 18. The wrecking ball approacheth. The reader may recall that the replacement storage shed (bright red!) is already in place nearby. The new shed will clearly not embrace cat habitation; the door is always closed tightly, and the underneath area is screened off from entry.

Will the new kittens who live underneath the old shed even survive the tearing-down process? They are so small that they need but a tiny horizontal crack along the bottom through which to dive and from which to emerge. And where will the feral cats "live" when their home is gone? A number of kittens have been born and raised in that space under the old shed. (There must be a larger entryway somewhere at the bottom of a hidden part of a side or back wall of this shed.) It is safe most of the time (well, except when poison is brought into play). Where will they go during thunderstorms? Where can they sleep protected and warm? The old white storage shed! It has been dependable and familiar to them. It has been a home. How can this happen, and in this way? To tear down homes and then fail to provide new ones for the ousted inhabitants is a grievous offense indeed.

Saturday, September 18, 2010

Early this afternoon I stopped by the parking lot to see what had happened with the old storage shed. It was completely gone. The men who had taken it down were just then starting to drive away in their truck. I stopped them to chat about it. They said they had seen absolutely no evidence of cats underneath the shed. No evidence whatsoever.

Sunday, September 26, 2010

It has been eight days and counting since the feral cat "home" was torn down. I haven't seen hide nor hair of any feral cat in the parking lot area since their shed was demolished. I haven't visited the area to offer any food to any cat since the destruction of their home on September 18. Is *home* the correct term, the correct usage of the word "home"? Is it better to say their *place,* their *hideout,* or their *hangout?*

The ferals' familiar parking lot territory is now drastically changed. The new red storage shed has sturdy, tight fencing at the bottom, prohibiting creatures from entering the space underneath the structure. There is a high, strong fence around the trash dumpsters next to it, which will surely keep animals away. It's all very clean, strong, and efficient—and harshly unaccommodating to any animal seeking shelter, warmth and coziness, protection, dryness, and tidbits of windfall food. Maybe this is to be considered progress? For one thing, because of the improved sightlines, it is now easier to keep a better eye on, and to keep track of, the crowds of children who by day inhabit the buildings on this campus and who play on the surrounding outdoor playgrounds. This is a good thing. And a garden bed is to be installed in the area of the old shed for the children to plant and tend. And a pavilion is to be built at that site for the purpose of outdoor education. Applaudable, no doubt, and very exciting. But I hope we haven't lost, in the process of these developments, another source of valid outdoor education: the ferals.

There is one exception regarding my statements at the beginning of this section known as September 26, 2010. That would be the omnipresent Caramel of course. Caramel does continue to hang about, but sadly, looking thin lately. I've seen ribs poking out against the orange sides of this persevering, valiant (and perhaps challenged) little animal.

Sunday, October 3, 2010

OK, fifteen days and counting. My resolve to leave the ferals alone is weakening. If it hadn't been raining, I would have gone to the parking lot tonight to see if they (=Caramel) are still around (=could be fed).

Wednesday, November 3, 2010

I spotted a black kitten dashing speedily across the dark parking lot as I emerged from the adjacent main building, having worked late. I went back inside to find cat food, and when I came out to the lot, no cat was in sight. After a while, I called, "Silky! Come on, Silky! Come on, baby! Silkeeee!" At which Caramel appeared.

Caramel started meowing loudly at me. I took the food and water bowls to a spot hidden from view, and almost immediately, Caramel and a black kitten emerging from underneath a nearby parked bus pounced on the food together. I provided copious amounts. Caramel seemed in good, healthy shape.

I had spotted a black kitten right by the side of the road nearby, last night on the way to choir practice, and I was sad that there was no way to get food to the little cat. This kitten needs a name, don't you think? And a name for its twin as well. I don't know. I think I may be getting confused. I suppose Blacky will do.

Later in November 2010

One evening, after I called "Silkee . . . SILKEEEE!" four cats appeared: Starlight, Young Starlight, Caramel, and Little Caramel. After initial aggressive pushing and shoving at the site of the food bowls, the little group ate hungrily and quickly, but peacefully, together. But it seems a dog's chance that I'll ever see Silky again. Why isn't SHE showing up here?

Even later in November 2010

As I was fixing to go home after working late this evening, I saw Little Caramel calmly reclining right in the middle of the parking lot next to my car! S/he showed a similar M.O. to his/her (presumable) parent, Caramel—an in-your-face demeanor, a no-hiding but instead out-in-the-open presence, meaning to be seen. The other cats, on the other hand, always conceal themselves behind or half-behind something, lying in wait while blending in with the environment.

Wednesday, January 12, 2011

"O most courageous day! O most happy hour!" (Again from Shakespeare's *A Midsummer Night's Dream*)—Silky! I had a Silky encounter late this afternoon! What a thrill—it was the first such occurrence in a very long time. The circumstances were uncannily similar to the occasion of March 3, 2010.

Exiting my workplace, I used a door I don't normally use—the front door next to the full, round holly bush earlier referred to as location C. A black cat, lurking in the shadow of a corner where the wide entryway meets the front wall of the building, suddenly bolted out at me. Startling me, grabbing my full attention. This cat meowed piteously at me. Had it approached everyone who exited by that door this afternoon, and in such a bold manner? Or was it ME for whom this cat was waiting, angling? If so, how did this beloved cat think I might use this particular doorway?

This very area is where I lured and trapped Silky a year and a half ago; it is near where she brought her kittens, near Cat Haven; it's exactly where she found me for food on March 3, 2010.

The gorgeous thing stared steadily at me—right into my eyes—with a penetrating, mesmerizing look. The eyes were bright and dazzling. Silky's eyes. As is her usual attitude toward me, she was nervous, skittish—much more so than the other cats are. And the holly bush location, it's where she got food from me last March when she was desperately hungry. Also, it's away from the area near the buses' parking spaces and the new red storage shed where I have been feeding the ferals lately and where that gang knows to gather in order to obtain food from me. Silky is not a regular in that parking lot gang. Silky would do her own thing, not gather with a familiar gang in a usual spot. This cat was not doing the usual drill to obtain food; this cat was showing an unusual approach to getting food from me. Silky's M.O.

There wasn't much time to produce a bowl of food for Silky: a) people could appear on the scene at any moment, and b) Caramel could appear on the scene at any moment. Fortunately, I had food available, so I brought it right out and placed it under the holly bush. Silky located it quickly and feasted upon it.

In short order, a striped tan/orange cat steadily approached—Little Caramel. I didn't worry about any Johnny-come-lately stealing Silky's food though. Silky holds her own; other cats quickly learn from her body language not to interfere with her dining.

Silky's action of coming right up to the occupied building, a place with lots of potential danger and unwelcoming vibes for a wild animal (a feral cat for instance), actually worked well because it is the darkest time of the year, with early evenings and nights so dark and murky, with shadows so deeply black, that a black cat cannot be noticed. You would have to stare very hard to detect this crinose, creeping, crawling, crafty creature crouched under the large holly bush, quietly eating dinner. So, profoundly black Silky made it very easy for me to pull off a feeding with no one detecting my (frowned upon) actions. Then I went to the far edge of the parking lot and fed the usual gang.

Thursday, January 13, 2011

A large-ish group of kittens and cats appeared around me as I went to my car to go home from work at 7:30 p.m. To be fed. This is probably not a good scenario. The parking lot feral cat gang is expanding, and I don't even know the names of many of these cats. I just don't recognize most of them anymore. I think things are getting out of hand.

I was recently informed about the existence of Alley Cat Allies. This outfit operates the "trap, neuter, and release" program, which is apparently the best way to deal with feral cats. Should I try to utilize the organization with regard to my parking lot feral cats? In order to accomplish this, though, I would be bringing a spotlight to bear on the thriving feral cat presence at my workplace, which the administration would presumably not welcome. Engendering negative publicity? And it would probably cost some money—it should cost money because it's a valuable service. And perhaps I would be accused of encouraging the feral cats to appear on the campus grounds; I do value my job there, and I don't want to be considered a "problem" or an odd "cat lady." (Just wait until they read this book.) On the other hand, could this be a valuable environmental education project of which the children who populate the building and campus could be made aware? They could benefit from learning the best way to handle a feral cat colony. Engendering positive publicity?

Monday, January 24, 2011

Tonight, as I prepared to leave the workplace at 5:45 (nightfall in winter!), Caramel approached me, meowing. I got into my car, where I had food at the ready. Yes, I was secretly hoping to see my cat acquaintances tonight because I've missed them. Caramel sat down nearby to watch me, or rather to wait for me to produce the goodies, absolutely sure that I would do just that. Starlight soon joined Caramel, and they sat together quietly and patiently near my car. Lovebirds? Proud parents? Domestic bliss? Or just plain fellow fighters for survival?

I can't resist feeding them. How can I? Today, the temperature outside didn't rise above the twenties. Below freezing. Can the cats find enough food? Aaargh! At this time of year, food for them must be as scarce as hens' teeth. I must say, though, Caramel and Starlight do look healthy—not too thin or scrawny.

Anyway, I walked with the food bowl toward the parked buses. Starlight made a beeline to the location I have been utilizing mostly lately, against one of the concrete boundary markers at the far end of the bus parking spaces, out of sight, and very dark and covered. Caramel, however, got right into my path, as s/he has done once or twice before, facing me with a ferocious-looking stance—front paws spread apart, head low, eyes intensely glaring. It seems quite threatening! Is it mock play or in earnest? "Excuse me," I say. "May I pass?" Caramel allows me to advance a few steps, then again with the attack-mode pose or whatever. What is that all about? Wildness. It bemuses me. And it brings a smile.

I gave Caramel and Starlight their own separate bowls—gigantic helpings—and Caramel actually stayed with the one bowl, rather than make repeated runs to check out what the other bowl held. As they dined, a very young cat—almost still a kitten—showed up. This young 'un sported a white coat with splotches of shaded browns and grays. I would want to call this cat Patches, but I've already named a bigger, similarly colored cat I've seen around here Patches.

What if someone else is feeding these cats on a regular basis? What if this person has already given names to these cats? Well anyway, these names I've given the ferals are just for my own purposes. As for them, they all respond to being called Silky.

I've learned of a neighbor who lives a short distance down the road from my workplace, in fact, who feeds a colony of feral cats on a regular basis. Amazing. Who would care? These cats are free to roam wherever they please throughout the surrounding rural countryside. This lady is Mrs. Share Moresun. Mrs. Moresun has actually employed Alley Cat Allies very successfully to help with her feral cats, and I heard that they humane-captured thirty-one cats, which were then neutered and released! That seems like quite a feat and an admirable accomplishment. I really can't imagine how it was done.

Tuesday, February 1, 2011

Driving to work today, I saw, sad to say, a young cat lying dead in the middle of the road, frozen, gravely injured, but all stretched out in graceful repose. The coat was black, decorated with rich brown streaky patches. Looked to be a pretty little thing with a delicate, completely black head and face. Oh my. I will call this cat Sable de Luxe. S/he was killed so near to my workplace that I suppose s/he must have been a member of the parking lot ferals. Or Share Moresun's ferals? Are these two cat gangs one and the same?

Thursday, February 3, 2011

Driving to work today, I saw, sad to say, that the head of Sable de Luxe had been almost completely severed from the body. I suppose this was done by vehicles driving over Sable in the middle of the road. Obviously, I would need to call the Humane Society to come to the scene and handle the remains of Sable de Luxe in a more genteel manner. Before I got a chance to call, however, I noticed later on that Sable de Luxe's body was gone.

Saturday, February 12, 2011

I wish I could hunt Silky down, capture her, and keep her always near me. It would make me so happy to have Silky as a pet—to see her daily, take care of her, and interact with her on a regular basis, whenever I wanted to. I wonder how I could possibly accomplish this. How would it work? For instance, would she be an outdoor cat or an indoor cat? Could she be an indoor cat? Who will help me with the undertaking of this plan?

I know there is an undercurrent of Thoreau in all this, though I only vaguely sense it, and I don't yet understand it. I can't quite grasp it. But it feels very, very important. It has to do with the idea of a search—my search.

Thoreau tells us that he was on a search when he states the following:

> I seek acquaintance with Nature, to know her moods and manners. Primitive Nature is the most interesting to me. I take infinite pains to know all the phenomena of spring, for instance, thinking that I have here the entire poem, and then, to my chagrin, I learn that it is but an imperfect copy that I possess and have read, that my ancestors have torn out many of the first leaves and grandest passages, and mutilated it in many places. I should not like to think that some demigod had come before me and picked out some of the best of the stars. I wish to know an entire heaven and an entire earth.[17]

---

[17] Henry David Thoreau, Eliot Porter, *In Wildness is the Preservation of the World* (Oakland, CA: Sierra Club, 1962).

Monday, February 14, 2011

Today in the late afternoon, I caught sight of Silky. She had climbed up onto the lowest branches of a huge shrub opposite the large, dense holly bush of location C. A casual passerby would probably not have noticed the silent black cat, perfectly still, among the branches and foliage. But the burning, bright yellow orbs of her eyes, staring straight ahead, perfectly round and standing out in the surrounding darkness—wouldn't that pair of eyes be seen by passersby?

Happy as a peacock, I placed a bowl of yummy, moist canned food in a dark corner formed by two walls near the holly bush. I observed from the window right above that spot that Silky hungrily ate it all, then wanted more. A fresh bowl of dry food was next, but I didn't dare take the time so openly in view to set out a bowl of water. It was daylight, with people still in and around the building. *There is still plenty of snow around*, I reassured myself.

Soon Blacky appeared. Silky was not willing to share. Blacky had to wait patiently nearby to profit off of whatever might be left over. Caramel was not there at all.

Tuesday, February 15, 2011

A similar scene occurred today. No Caramel! Silky has cleverly managed to get food from me. She can obviously pick me out among the throngs of people who go in and out of the various buildings on campus all day. She is working a situation, a time and a location, targeted to her alone, of which the other cats aren't really aware. I believe this is intelligently, purposefully calculated on her part.

But how long until Caramel becomes aware of the new feeding plan, and horns in? Therefore, I (and my cat food) must make myself scarce for the next few days. Or else the jig will be up, the solo Silky show will be over, and the cat-feeding scenario will bloom into something unmanageable and undesirable, devolving into a situation where a number of cats appear in a central and obvious area at 3:30 or 4:00 p.m. (carpool time!), milling around the cars and waiting to be fed. What a kettle of fish that would be. I must protect my "under the radar" private and close encounters with my cat, Silky.

I planned to lay low for the next few days, clear the air. I was willing to bet that Silky and I would then reconnect at the same time and location on some future day . . . and then come up with a new plan . . . of some kind . . . maybe . . .

*   *   *

Do you ever go on a quest? Or rather, do you ever FIND your-self going on a quest? And is the object of your quest elusive, somewhat hard to grasp? Is that element perhaps in the defini-tion of the word "quest"? And maybe BECAUSE the goal is hard to reach, is the striving, and is what occurs along the path toward that goal, just as important (or even more important) as the goal itself? I propose that it is.

Think of Don Quixote's Dulcinea, for example. Who, or what, is Dulcinea? She is a pure and beautiful young woman called up out of Quixote's imagination in order to give himself a lady to fight for, as the chivalrous knight in shining armor from ancient legend about whom he has read with great relish. So he hops onto his old workhorse, puts on an antique suit of armor, attaches a cardboard visor to a helmet, and goes on an epic quest for the favor of his Lady Dulcinea, who is a glorious vision he simply evoked out of thin air. He aims to eliminate all evil and wickedness in the world in order to protect and save his damsel. This is a hopeless quest, taken on by an impossible knight-errant. I suggest, therefore, that what is of most interest and importance in the tale of Don Quixote are the things that happen to him along the way, the various events and activity that comprise his journey. Embrace the journey.

Another aspect of a quest, or rather of the journey toward the fulfillment of a quest, is described by John Matthews in *The Quest for the Green Man*: "As you go, do not be surprised if you find yourself accompanied, shadowed by the very being you are seeking."[18] Matthews asserts that as we hunt for something, it, s/he, also hunts us, until we no longer know who the hunter is and who is hunted. When we pursue something intently and relentlessly, we can find it actually pursuing us, tracking us, in turn! Does Silky pursue me, find ways of coming into contact with me? By now, it's clear to both my reader and to me that Silky does exactly that.

I have been studying books about the Green Man because I've connected the Green Man to my search for Silky. Earlier, I explained why (once I figured it out). I look for the Green Man, hoping and assuming he is prevailing. Because the quest for Silky brings us into the natural world, where the Green Man is.

Ages ago, when I was in my twenties, a man who was a renowned Country Dance researcher, instructor, and caller wrote the following words in a letter to me:

> You are one who is searching. Don't give up the search! The process is far more important than the goal. Sometimes confusion is the spice of life (particularly in dancing). One of the great revelations of my life occurred when I could say to myself, "I am one of

---

[18] John Matthews, *The Quest for the Green Man* (Wheaton, Illinois: Quest Books, 2001).

the weirdest people I know." No remorse, no shame. I bask in my weirdness, or is it uniqueness? It's nice to grow up without being entirely grown-up. "Maturity," Jonathan Winters once said, "is finding out you're just like everyone else."

So is "maturity" the goal? Is that REALLY what we want to achieve? And do I REALLY want to "capture" Silky? Patient reader, do you remember how I felt at the beginning of this story as I walked toward the cage with the captured Silky inside? I felt frightened, deeply troubled, discomposed—like "the world around me was coming to an end." I feared that I had captured and caged something, acquired something, that I ultimately did not wish to have conquered at all (like "maturity"). Perhaps Silky represents an element on our planet that should never be tampered with, never be cornered, subdued, conquered.

"Sometimes confusion is the spice of life." Here is yet another aspect of the quest, the search, the hunt, the journey, the path we tread—confusion, chaos. What Buddhist teachings mean by "the path" is the moment-by-moment evolution of our experience and of our thoughts and emotions. One of the things the venerable Chögyam Trungpa Rinpoche said about "the path" is this: "Whatever occurs in the confused mind is regarded as the path. Everything is workable. It is a fearless proclamation, the lion's roar." This same Buddhist teacher also said, "Chaos should be regarded as extremely good news." And Friedrich Nietzsche pointed out, "You must have chaos within you to give rise to a shining star." It's all about the path, the way, the journey (toward).

*   *   *

"Walk, Shepherdess, Walk"
by Eleanor Farjeon

Walk shepherdess walk
And I'll walk too
We'll find the ram with the ebony horns
And the gold footed ewe

The lamb with fleece of silver
Like summer sea foam
The wether with its golden bell
That leads them all home

So, walk shepherdess walk
And I'll walk too
And if we never find them
I sha'nt mind, shall you[19]

I used to think that the lines "And the wether with its golden bell /
That leads them all home" would make a perfectly adequate ending to this poem, quite a fine ending, really. It's not so much that
it's satisfying to end with a thought of reaching home, or even of
being led there by a sheep with a golden bell. It's because ending
with that line confirms that the intent of the walk is to find the
spectacular sheep made of things like gold, silver, and ebony, and
we won't stop until that intent is finally fulfilled. That's the goal;
that's what we intend to do—to acquire those treasures. In fact,
when I was little, I considered the last two lines of this poem,

---

[19] Eleanor Farjeon, "Walk, Shepherdess, Walk," lyrics found on The Mudcat Café,
accessed September 19, 2024, https://mudcat.org/thread.cfm?threadid=172251.

where the speaker tells the shepherdess, "And if we never find them, / I sha'n't mind, shall you?" to be a real bummer. I wanted the magical animals—and their gold and silver and ebony.

But those final two lines are there, and what a stunning question they ask us! Delightful! And thus, I finally realize the enlightening message of this poem—the walk itself is the goal; the walk itself is the success. So Farjeon's ending is totally on point, even more so than the glorious, envisioned animals she has called up, with their precious and valuable components! Embrace the journey.

Sunday, February 27, 2011

For the last two weeks, on several early evenings as I left work, I found that I was arranging things so as to actually avoid seeing the ferals. I had parked my car as far away from the new storage shed and bus parking area as possible; I tiptoed to my car, and then was thankful that I drove away undetected by the cat gang.

This, obviously, was a total change of attitude for me. Truthfully, I was in a hurry to get someplace else, or I was tired, or feeling under the weather and needed to go home and get right to bed.

Last Wednesday evening, I needed to rush to my ninety-one-year-old mother. She was in the hospital, having had another one of her "episodes." I was in a big hurry to be with her and to help take care of her, and the hospital was a long distance away. As I headed out of the parking lot, I turned to see, as they wandered near the new red storage shed and under the parked buses, two of the feral cats: Caramel and a black cat. Even though it was too dark to see which black cat was there, I could see all too clearly that both cats were hanging their heads low, and they seemed a bit defeated, downhearted. Both also looked a little thin, especially Caramel. That image haunted me for a while. But I didn't, couldn't, stop to feed them. People were around, and I was in a rush. I didn't have the time to wait until the people were gone so that the cat feeding could take place privately and unnoticed.

Thursday, March 3, 2011

Today in the late afternoon, I peered intently out of the window that looms just above the large holly bush of location C at my workplace. Yes, I was searching for Silky. And bingo, I found her there, sitting comfortably on all fours under the holly bush among the old, dark pieces of mulch and the dead leaves. I brought out bowls of food and water to her. She ate steadily and heartily, intent on her meal, until all of the food was gone. Then she sat under the full, thickly foliaged holly bush for quite a while, gazing straight ahead across the parking lot, or turning to fix me with a stare when I perchance made a sound at my window post.

Silky looked grand. She was plump and beautiful, and she looked healthy and strong, with her thick, dusky black coat. The telltale dash of stark white on her chest added an elegant touch of flair, and the two large, bright yellow, fathomless, round eyes were absolutely commanding—dazzling.

Hours later, I set out food and water at my more commonly used feeding location near the parked buses at the red storage shed. Caramel and the splotchy, patchy-coated kitten showed up from parts unknown. The patchy-coated kitten I will call Patchouli. Yes, Patchouli and not Patches, a name previously considered for this animal. Anyway, these cats didn't seem all that interested in the food I provided. There was no meowing, and the food was left unfinished so that I had to eventually discard it!

Both cats looked to be in excellent shape—clean, healthy, well filled-out. It struck me again how their coats display astonishingly beautiful coloring and handsome markings and patterns of design.

I believe Nature is supporting her animals, both wild and domesticated. That's why my feral cat parking lot gang can, and does, thrive. In the following classical song, we find a poetic description of the importance and benefits of trees.

"Ombra Mai Fu"
(an aria from *Xerxes*, an opera by George F. Handel,
with words, originally in Italian, by Silvio Stampiglia, after Nicolo Minato):

Xerxes:
(recitative) Tender and beautiful fronds
of my beloved plane tree
let Fate smile upon you.
May thunder, lightning, and storms
never disturb your dear peace,
nor may you by blowing winds be profaned.

(aria – Larghetto) Never was
a shade of any plant
dearer and more lovely
or more sweet.

The above words are a literal translation of the original language of the song, as found in *Classicalexburns*, an award-winning classical music blog by Alex Burns. And the aria is often sung by itself in English, using the following singable lyrics, which are a much looser translation:

Under your shade
green leaves now shelter me,
strong boughs lean over me,
moss for my bed.

* * *

Now here is a fascinating archetype: the Tree of Life. Some people have the image tattooed onto their bodies. I have seen a suggestion of the Tree of Life in that special tree at Cat Haven—to which I refer in this book as the "tall, gracious gift-giver of an evergreen tree" at the corner of a certain building on a certain rural campus.

* * *

The Green Man is a Wood Spirit, or Guardian of the Forests.

Wednesday, March 9, 2011

Ever since my observations on March 3, I have felt happy and relaxed, satisfied that the ferals are going to be fine, one way or the other, with or without me. For one thing, there's someone else around who is caring for them—that seems obvious to me. Others are looking out for their well-being. For another thing, they are "running the race hungry," so complacency and apathy aren't in their nature. These cunning creatures have strong senses, amazingly acute animal instincts, and a steep learning curve.

* * *

It's been months since I've seen any cats at all around my work-place. I haven't been able to do a single thing to encourage them either. I find that this dearth has been making me feel rather uncertain and melancholy. I had thought that maybe I was done with the whole cat thing, free of it, especially know-ing that they can thrive without me. But I realize now that I am not finished with it, and it has not finished with me. I need to continue my search for Silky—she continues to call me. And

I continue to have the feeling that one of the keys to finding Silky is to have the other cats around me.

Monday, November 14, 2011

Tonight, at about 6:30 (dark outside—night had fallen), as I was leaving in my car to go home, I spotted Patchouli at a grassy corner, right where s/he could clearly observe passing cars on the campus. "Oh joy, oh rapture unforeseen!" as the Gilbert and Sullivan chorus goes. But . . . Patchouli.

I turned to pull my car up near to the small cat, and immediately, s/he started meowing, as if recognizing the vehicle and who was driving, or at least realizing what the movement and slowing down of the car signified. Hope. It was the meowing of HOPE. The meows increased in frequency and excitement as, emerging from the car, I called out, "Silkeee, Silkeee, Siiilkeeee!"

I went inside the building and procured some dry cat food and fresh water in two bowls. The container of dry food had been sitting hidden in the back of my bottom desk drawer, half-forgotten, untouched for months. I could hear the meows as I stood INSIDE the building. Good grief, Patchouli, soft-pedal it, will you? I placed the bowls underneath a large shrub not far from Cat Haven, strongly hoping those two bowls were hidden from view. Because Bark's truck was in the parking lot!

I knew Patchouli was nearby, and I was trying to call him/her to the food, but s/he wouldn't go to the food as long as I was standing there; she hung back. When I walked away from the immediate area, s/he went ahead and ate the food.

There were a few stragglers (two-leggeds) about the place. I hope no one saw what I did with Patchouli. Finally, I got back into my car and headed home, and as I did so, the place was silent—no meowing—so I figured Patchouli was satisfied and pleasantly full of good food.

Friday, November 18, 2011

But of all cats to lead the charge, after the long lapse of parking lot feedings! Little Patchouli! I don't think I'll ever forget the sudden surprising sight several nights ago of Patchouli comfortably, but alertly and resolutely, reclining at the edge of that corner of the front lawn where several driveways meet, waiting and watching and being sure to BE SEEN. It was just early nightfall, and a number of vehicles with adults and children inside were passing to and fro.

I remember that Patchouli used to hang back while the other cats dug into the food I set out for them. Patchouli had seemed vague and unsure, even unable. I had wondered if Patchouli was intimidated by the other cats. Patchouli's behavior was always different from the other cats—Patchouli was slower moving and not at all a noticeable presence, just a quiet, shy shadow blending into the background of vehicles, shrubs, and small outbuildings. Patchouli was a fussy eater as well. S/he eschewed the canned, moist delicacies and would only eat the dry pellets.

So this night, I, forgetting myself in an inexcusable manner, offered a bowl of canned "turkey parts" in dark gravy to Patchouli. The meowing continued until I brought out a bowl of dry food.

Later, as I went to my car to go home, I spied Patchouli sitting at Cat Haven. I spoke many soothing sounds, and Patchouli listened quietly. We kept our distance but made a nice little connection between us, a nice little tableau. Patchouli didn't bolt away but seemed happy to linger there at Cat Haven.

Friday, January 13, 2012

5:45 p.m.

Very dark, bitter cold, and the place had been basically deserted for the night. As I exited the building using the doorway near to both Cat Haven (to my left) and the holly bush of location C (to my immediate right), I saw Patchouli on the edge of the pavement, seeming to be engaged in an altercation or standoff with another meowing cat hidden from sight in the low shrubbery near Patchouli.

I went back inside to obtain food and fresh water and placed it in two long-standing dark-colored glassware bowls under the huge shrub opposite the large, dense holly bush of location C. Shortly, I observed a black cat at the food bowl. Patchouli was hanging back, looking askance. I went back inside and then brought out another black glass bowl I happened to have handy, full of dry food (to appeal to Patchouli's palate), and placed it under the holly bush, and Patchouli went over there and ate from that bowl.

The black cat had been very effective at claiming the "feeding area" and at obtaining dibs on the first bowl of food to appear. I was obviously very interested in this black cat, and after a little while, I had a face-to-face encounter with the creature on the dimly lit sidewalk pavement. As I live and breathe, here was Silky. Here she was. This fabulous black animal showed the ferocity of my precious Silky, also the burning intensity in the eyes, also the exact voice: thin, clear, expressive, high-toned (but not shrill), it was plaintive, resounding, captivating, CALLING, making one highly desirous to know what exactly she's saying. This voice goes "through me like an arrow" (to borrow an expression from artist Robert Motherwell). Yes, and "Sweet, piercing sweet was the music of Pan's pipe" (a caption under a depiction of Pan by Walter Crane). Must nurture that precious voice. Must purchase new cans of moist cat food for her.

Saturday, January 14, 2012

Early in the evening, I visited the exact area where I had spotted Silky last evening. Hoping for another encounter (I'm in a perpetual state of hoping for another encounter.), I put all of my senses on high alert. There was still some food left in both bowls. I heard mewing and scanned the garden for the cat making the sound. It took a little while, but I finally discerned Patchouli hunkered down on the ground among several low shrubs. S/he made no move, neither up toward where I was nor toward the food and water bowls. Was s/he positioned there for the night or for some indefinite period? Did s/he not care for leftovers? Or was s/he guarding the food supply at the usual feeding time, guarding it from oh, say, SILKY? Patchouli was just, maybe, simply . . . there.

I drove away, but for the rest of the night, I wondered if I should bring Patchouli a blanket in which to cozy up. It was to be a frigid night out there. I decided not to provide a blanket, not to add anything besides food to the scene, to the environment with which Patchouli must deal. I don't know if I'm happy with that decision.

Sunday, January 15, 2012

Late this morning, I stopped by the feeding area I had visited last night. Oh I of little faith wanted to see whether or not Patchouli had perished in the freezing temperature of last night in that little spot among the low shrubs where s/he had chosen to repose. Patchouli was not there. There was plenty of dried mulch, dead leaves of all sizes, evergreen foliage, rocks, bits of paper, windblown odds and ends of discarded stuff. Plenty of windbreaks. Could one make do with those things on a bitterly freezing-cold night? The spot was protected, covered nicely, and a good hiding place. Cats have warm fur coats. The food bowls were empty; I refilled the bowls, left the scene, and went home.

Wednesday, April 25, 2012

Tonight, I worked late. Then at 7:15, I went out to the parking lot to go home. I was thinking that I hadn't done much for the cats in a long while, that my efforts had been minimal for the last several months, and that I hadn't seen them around for quite a while, least of all Silky. I was thinking, well, they're just plain gone from here. Just have to accept that. Let them go. Silky too, then. At that very moment I saw Silky next to my car. But how incredible! 'Twould seem that fate has fantasticated here! A fantasy come alive and real!

As I approached my car, she did the Silky bolt over to the tall evergreen at the corner of the main building where I had first seen her as she watched over her brood of four little kittens several years ago. The two bright, glowing, yellow eyes fixed me with a riveting, ferocious glare. I stared back in fascination. Finally, I gave the Silky call: "Silkee, Siiilkeee, Siiilkeeee!" She responded immediately, meowing her insistent, galvanizing cry. We were having a real conversation! Silky obviously recognized and responded to my voice. Apparently, she knows my car too.

Continually meowing, she traveled through the garden to the very spot where I had last seen her several months ago. I set out a bowl of dried cat treats nearby, of several kinds, but when

I returned with a bowl of fresh water, she was utterly gone, having eaten just a small portion of the treats.

Silky was very skittish tonight. She carried herself in a low, prowling manner, looking nervous and intimidating at the same time. She kept her head low, which seemed both a menacing and a defensive posture to me.

She didn't look like a picture of health, although this was only a general impression, because she kept hiding from me and I could not get a good look at her. Her coat was OK, I guess, but seemed a bit dull, without its former sheen. She looked a tad lean and lank. I could be wrong, but it just looked like she didn't feel well. Her appetite was low? She was not at all in a serene, content state. She was very active, on high alert—certainly far from lethargic, though. I don't know the signs. I guess I can understand why she dashes away from me and hides from me, but she also knows how to find me for food and fresh water.

Saturday, April 28, 2012

For the past few days since I saw Silky, and even on occasion for a few days before I saw her, I had set out a bowl of dry food with a bowl of water near location C. More often than not, when I collected the bowls later, the dry food had not been touched—I brought back with me bowls still completely full of food. This trend is definitely a big change from former days, something new. Occasionally, one new cat does appear on the scene to eat some food—just this one, and this cat I do not know. S/he is white with a few orange patches (like "pork chops" as they would be called by a tattoo artist). This cat looks domesticated and gentle. It's a big, plump cat, and slow-moving.

Where on earth has THIS creature come from? Where is s/he going?

Sunday, May 19, 2013 (about a year later)

This morning at church, Mrs. Moresun excitedly informed me that she had seen Silky yesterday! Silky showed up around 4:00 p.m. to eat from the food bowl Mrs. Moresun sets out at the front of her home down the road from me, under the eave of their huge barn-sized garage. Mrs. Moresun, of course, loves the local feral cats and knows how to manage them. We would discuss the feral cats after church from time to time, sharing information about them.

Oh joy! Christmas comin' again! Got some happy news! She did! Now we're cookin' with peanut oil! Great day in the morning! Happy as a flea in a doghouse! Buzzing! It has been ages since I've seen Silky, though I think of her often. I told Mrs. Moresun I had given up hope of encountering Silky ever again, presuming her dead and gone from this world. "Oh, no!" Mrs. Moresun responded. "Never give up. Don't ever give up." She seemed surprised and dismayed that I would even have such a thought.

Later, my husband who lives across the river shared during a phone conversation that at the auto mechanic shop where he works, some of the men have enjoyed the presence of two or three feral cats who hang around the garage. These men feed the cats regularly and have even purchased a cat "igloo" for them (whatever that is).

At 3:30 this afternoon, I went over to the Moresun house, and Mr. and Mrs. Moresun welcomed me gladly and were more than fine with me sitting on their lawn searching for

Silky. Both of the Moresuns were outside doing garden and lawn work, so Mrs. Moresun took a moment to point out to me that Silky (as opposed to the usual denizens) would not come around their close-at-hand human presence comfortably, but would tend to hide and lurk, nearby but under cover. This particular attempt to see Silky didn't pan out, but Mrs. Moresun chatted amiably about the local feral cats and their behaviors. She told me that there are four cats that come regularly to the food she sets out—the "queen" is Georgia. There was a pause while Mrs. Moresun tried to remember the name of the next one, at which point Mr. Moresun, a hefty, handsomely sun-wizened man, entered the conversation with "Fluffy!" Oh yes, there's also Precious, a gray cat, and Baby-face, an all-black cat.

Mrs. Moresun said Silky is elusive. (No kidding!) She shows up after long periods of absence. Again, not news to me. *Absent from you, absent from me,* I thought, *so present WHERE?* Silky eats some food, stares intently at Mrs. Moresun, and then bolts. Sounds 'bout right, doesn't it? An unpredictable mystery.

Mrs. Moresun spoke further: She knows the route they take across meadows and then through a woodsy area to get to her house (from, say, the direction of the campus where I work); it's all well back from the road. Also, she has seen the cats walking single file together down to the railroad tracks, one of their favorite hunting grounds because there they can catch mice or moles; they're cats, they hunt. All of them keep to themselves and won't be touched by humans, and they keep their distance, but they sure know how and where to get food.

Don't give up. Don't ever give up.

Saturday, May 25, 2013

3:30 p.m.

I sat (in my car) in the Moresuns' driveway. What a beautiful place they have—gardens galore, perfectly lovely trees and many of them, their beauty made livelier today by a stiff wind blowing their leafy branches to and fro, shrubbery of different kinds. Searching for Silky, I saw Fluffy.

Also, I saw that I was parked next to a big yellow bus! (Just like before when I used to see cats at the campus where I work) (Share Moresun drives a school bus on weekdays.) I recalled the report that Silky was actually the first one to the feeding at 4:00 p.m. here a week ago, HERE AT THIS SPOT. Just down the road a little way from the farm where I'm living, practically just across the street!

Oh! I saw a smallish black cat with huge bright eyes, glowing yellow! I quickly had an urgent conference with Mrs. Moresun, whereupon this cat was identified as Babyface. This cat had a small face like Silky's, but s/he didn't have the carriage and general demeanor of Silky at all. Babyface seemed too at ease and at home here to be identified as Silky.

There was more discussion with Share regarding the behavior of the four cats that currently hang out here. Feedings at 4:30 p.m., not 4:00. And Share said that she had not seen Silky around her house since the sighting a week ago.

How can I connect with Silky at this point? As truly welcoming as they are, I really shouldn't keep intruding, barging onto the Moresuns' property to just sit and stare, should I? I believe the proper term is "loitering" . . . Should I start setting out food again at the building where I work nearby? Should I obtain one of Silky's offspring to own? I could probably track some of them down—I'm thinking of Barny, Smoky, Cooky, and Joe.

Thursday, May 30, 2013

This evening at 7:30, there was a performance of a geography play outside in the recreation area next to the parking lot of my workplace. I was playing musical instruments to help things along. Then the crowd entered the building to view the Famous Explorers exhibit. My part having been finished, I climbed into my car to go home.

My car had been parked so that the front windshield offered a view of a distant hedge line in front of a long fence. The time of year, time of day, and weather conditions all reminded me of an occasion three years ago when I had found myself compelled to stare at that same distant fence with hedges and tall grass growing beside it. I was forced to stop and stare now.

My eyes discerned a small, pitch-black shape that was an unexpected part of the landscape. It didn't look like a shadow or a dark stump or anything like that, and it was a solid deep-black color of a vaguely interesting and appealing shape. The situation certainly bore further investigation. I fixed my eyes on the shape, and lo and behold, it moved! It moved along the ground a short distance and then, slowly, some more.

Several cars were still parked in the lot, but since no one was actually around at that moment, I got out of my car and yelled, "Silkeeee . . . Silky! Silky!" A thin, high-pitched meow immediately answered my call. The next thing I knew, the black thing, which I now saw was a cat, had crossed the field toward me halfway and was sitting bolt upright in the middle of the field, staring my way with bright yellow-orange eyes! I made a beeline for the building, grabbed some paper picnic plates off of the refreshment table, went inside, and got some cat food and fresh water. When I emerged and set down the food and water for this alluring black cat, s/he was gone. I called and called, to no avail. I went here and there indecisively—excited, but not sure what to do next.

Finally, I headed for the building, aiming to use the front entrance at location C near Cat Haven and where the broad, sturdy holly bush is. As I came to the wide concrete entryway, I softly spoke Silky's name to myself. Immediately came a high-pitched, plaintive meow-response, over and over again, practically from right underneath me, from the group of nearby low shrubs. I placed the food and water near that spot, and then wandered around some more, pretending to be talking on my cell phone. I saw no sign of a cat until, just as the cleaning man emerged with his cart, a black cat dashed between some cars, then just simply disappeared.

Well, sir, time to take a break and get some supper; also, the crowd from the evening's festivities was starting to flow out into the parking lot to leave for the night. So I drove to a takeout place, obtained my supper, and returned directly to the scene—at about 9:00 p.m.

At that time, the place was deserted. Everyone, cleaning crew included, had gone away. I got out of my car and saw a black cat sitting in the grass near the parking lot, in the shadow of a small incline. Aha! The cat, seeming to be waiting for me, got up immediately and approached me. I retrieved the food and water from near the wide concrete entryway where I found it untouched, except invaded by two slugs. I got rid of the slugs, and then set it out on the parking lot. The cat skittishly and warily, hissing now and then, went to the food and ate.

The water in the cup seemed to frighten this wild, nervous animal. Temperature not right? Smells wrong? Who knows.

After eating quite a bit of the food, s/he was satisfied. Then lots of loud meowing started. This cat seemed very interested in me. S/he kept a certain, consistent distance (about nine feet) as s/he circled around me, stopping sometimes to lie down and do cat things (bathing, rolling on the pavement, stretching, listening, reacting to sounds). There was a great deal of lurking at my car—s/he was very interested in it, a new car by the way. Maybe s/he was getting to know it. Am I being absurd?

I finally got a chance to look carefully at the cat when I managed to angle her into the light from a lot lamp and confirmed that yes, it was Silky, my precious joy, my completion. There was the small, triangular face, the tiny white patch high on her chest, and those amazing lighted eyes. She kept her head low and was wary and extremely alert. She is lithe and lean, but not too thin. She is now a medium-sized cat. Her coat is glossy and full and beautiful.

Silky and I spent an hour together, 9:00–10:00 p.m., in the parking lot near Cat Haven. We conversed. She meowed loudly and repeatedly. She seemed to have important things to say to me. At times, it seemed as if she was complaining and scolding vehemently, "Where have you been all this long time?" Well, Missy, I could say the same to you! When that eased up, I would simply say her name, and she would answer me immediately. The hissing had stopped. I of course was fascinated by all of this, and in a state of serene, blissful delight, on cloud nine. I dare to state that Silky was excited and happy to see me as well.

For a while, Silky ruled the parking lot absolutely, and then finally glided underneath a nearby bush and seemed to vanish into thin air. I saw no more bright eyes, nothing stirred, and when I called her name, there was no longer an answering meow.

I looked around me, searching for Silky, and saw, hovering everywhere above a big field across the nearby road, a host of brightly lit gamboling fireflies! Their lights seemed to have come directly from Silky's eyes—her abounding light can be shared endlessly—bright yellow, fiery brilliance that incites your imagination and draws you in, fascinated.

Guessing that we were done here, I got into my car and drove home to a late, now-cold supper. I felt uplifted and deeply satisfied for quite a while after this lengthy face-to-face with Silky. Once again, I thought of the lines from Browning's poem, "Pippa's Song": "God's in his heaven, / All's right with the world." Wildness is still out there somewhere; that glorious natural element still exists, not yet crushed by the dull, heavy weight of concrete and steel, or stifled by the sharp leveling blade of the mower.

So, for tonight, it's "Fairy's lullaby" for me, a whimsical poem by Katharine Lee Bates (also the writer of "America the Beautiful"). Here's how I'll imagine myself:

> In lily cup I'll nest me,
> From fairy dance to rest me . . .
>
> And the star-sprites lean above me,
> For all the star-sprites love me;
>> In circle fair
>> Each holds in air
> His small gold torch above me.[20]

---

[20] Katharine Lee Bates, excerpts from "Fairy's lullaby," a poem appearing in Fairy Gold (New York: E.P. Dutton & Co., 1916).

Could the star-sprites of Bates's poem be fireflies—
THOSE fireflies—holding little gold torches above fairies
sleeping, tired from their dance, in their nest-like flower cups,
gently rocked by the "wind-elf" as suggested in a later portion
of the poem?

And consider the lights way above us, the brilliance of the
fiery sparkles we see in the night sky. I like how Carl Sandburg
compares flowers to stars in his poem "There Are Different
Gardens." "The closing and speaking lips of the lily and the
warning of the fire and the dust—they are in the gardens and
the sky of stars."

Saturday, June 1, 2013

Early this evening, I showed up at the parking lot of my
workplace armed with cat food (dry and wet), fresh water,
and several cat toys. I watched and waited for Silky for quite
a while. I called and called. All to no avail. No Silky there
during that time.

But there were lots and lots of birds—more numerous than
fleas on a dog's back. They were at their evensong, and the chorus of birds singing strongly and melodiously was beautiful to
hear. Alleluia! It sounded like a canticle Saint Francis of Assisi
would have them sing, a song simply full of joyful praise:

From "Canticle Of The Sun" by Saint Francis of Assisi,
translation by Matthew Arnold:

Praised be my Lord God with all His creatures; and
specially our brother the sun, who brings us the day,
and who brings us the light; fair is he, and shining
with a very great splendour.

Praised be my Lord for our sister the moon, and for
the stars the which He has set clear and lovely in
heaven.

Praised be my Lord for our brother the wind, and for
air and cloud, calms and all weather, by the which
Thou upholdest in life all creatures.

Praised be my Lord for our sister water, who is very
serviceable unto us, and humble, and precious, and
clean.

Praised be my Lord for our brother fire, through
whom Thou givest us light in the darkness; and he
is bright and pleasant, and very mighty, and strong.

Praised be my Lord for our mother the earth, the
which doth sustain us and keep us, and bringeth forth
divers fruits, and flowers of many colours, and grass.[21]

So, perhaps the outing was worth it just for that, never
mind Silky?

Terry Tempest Williams said, "Once upon a time . . .
there was the simple understanding that to sing at dawn and to
sing at dusk was to heal the world through joy. The birds still
remember what we have forgotten, that the world is meant to
be celebrated."

* * *

Emmet is a cat belonging to the family who, not too long ago,
moved into the farmhouse next door. Emmet is black with a

---

[21] From "Canticle of the Sun" by Saint Francis of Assisi, translation by Matthew Arnold.

small white bib and big, bright, yellow eyes. So Emmet appears these days in my path (or even at my front door) looking like Silky but not being Silky. Aaargh! Harsh. It feels like a taunt, and it causes me great annoyance and displeasure—and, of course, disappointment. It's very pesky of Emmet to often appear around my home, lurking as if smirking, staring me down as if boldly sneering at me. And of course, it gives me pause every single time, causing me a quick moment of joyous excitement, which then dissolves right away into disgust.

* * *

One time, Emmet was lying right on top of a railing on my small front porch, relaxed and gazing leisurely about. The nerve. It was outrageous. Another time, I saw Emmet do something unseemly into a nearby newly planted asparagus patch. Here was a lovingly tended garden plot blessed with fresh young asparagus sprouts, and Emmet contaminated it, using it as his own personal litter box. Then he dug and scratched and scraped at the dirt on top. Gross. I could only turn away, shaking my head. I mean, REALLY!

* * *

But wait. A descriptive phrase I recently used for Silky has come into the spotlight in my mind, grabbing my attention and dominating the memory of my latest encounter with Silky. It's really bugging me. It's the "rolling on the pavement" on which I keep focusing. Silky seemed seized with the urge to roll around on the parking lot pavement, over and over, every which way, in disorganized fashion. Is this normal cat behavior? Is she just having a high ol' time? Is this a way to have fun? Is it "healthy cat" behavior?

On the other hand, is something bothering Silky? Could it be a sign of a health issue or of some sort of irritation or discomfort Silky is feeling? Or is that just me jumping to conclusions and completely misinterpreting her movements?

So maybe my new goal regarding Silky should be this: humane-trap her (again), and bring her to Mrs. Vet (again) to be checked for bothersome critters, cleaned of those pests, blood-tested for diseases (again), and treated for whatever might ail her. How can I manage to accomplish that (again)? Can I? Should I? Should I try?

Where is Silky?

"Wild thing, you make my heart sing, you make everything groooooovy, wild thing."[22]

* * *

Silky represents something valuable. In searching so intently for her, I have come to feel that I'm searching for wildness, true wildness. So Silky represents wildness.

Doesn't Max in Maurice Sendak's *Where the Wild Things Are* go on a similar search of his own? Why these searches? What set Max off on his journey to the "wild things"? How about the notion that Max was going to find wildness in order to, well, in order for SOMETHING—to accomplish something. What? Perhaps to come to terms with wildness, to accept it, to accept the wildness within himself, to befriend it, to live with it, in harmony, to make it OK WITH us, to embrace it. To master it? I don't know. Or perhaps it's simply that Max knew, and believed, Henry David Thoreau's words from *Walden*:

---

[22] "Wild Thing," song lyrics written by American composer James Wesley Voight-Wes Voight (a.k.a. Chip Taylor), originally recorded and released in 1965.

We need the tonic of wildness, to wade sometimes in marshes where the bittern and the meadow-hen lurk, and hear the booming of the snipe; to smell the whispering sedge where only some wilder and more solitary fowl builds her nest, and the mink crawls with its belly close to the ground. At the same time that we are earnest to explore and learn all things, we require that all things be mysterious and unexplorable, that land and sea be infinitely wild, unsurveyed and unfathomed by us because unfathomable. We can never have enough of nature. We must be refreshed by the sight of inexhaustible vigor, vast and titanic features, the sea-coast with its wrecks, the wilderness with its living and its decaying trees, the thunder cloud, and the rain which lasts three weeks and produces freshets. We need to witness our own limits transgressed, and some life pasturing freely where we never wander.[23]

So where are Sendak's wild things? It's suggested that they are right there, in Max's room with him. The forest is in Max's bedroom—along with an ocean, and the place "where the wild things are."

But Max traveled through time to find the wild things. I am one who hopes the place "where the wild things are" is not too remote. I hope we don't have to travel far. I hope we don't have to travel through time—either forward or backward—to find the wildness. But maybe we do. But I hope not.

---

[23] Henry David Thoreau, *Walden* (Boston: Ticknor and Fields, 1854).

Is our childhood a time and place of wildness? Is our childhood a joyous and wild "rumpus"? Is that why we need a mom? Do we need a mom? Max did. Children are primitive beings. Before my grandchild Ava R. Taylor could say words, she did roar and growl with joyful abandon when she saw the pictures of Sendak's wild beasts in *Where the Wild Things Are*.

The case that holds the movie version of *Where the Wild Things Are* states that there's a "wild thing" in each of us. In all seriousness, is that where we find wildness?

As my faithful and patient reader knows, one of the things I have discovered in my search for Silky is that there is a feral cat population. Where are the wild things? They are literally right here under our noses—but hidden among the low-lying shrubbery, trees, rocks, dumpsters, and small outbuildings. I had no idea. They're right HERE. Wildness seems to be all around us and even in us but undercover. AND I'm guessing it can't be totally squelched.

What is "wild thing" behavior? *Where the Wild Things Are* describes wildness as any or all of, but probably not limited to, the following: wrecking, chaos, willful destruction, smashing, biting, licking, howling, building a fortress, clawing, war is fun, battling is fun, tearing off limbs, eating each other, roaring, throwing dirt clods, out of control, causing injury. Also, dancing with abandon as in Max's command, "Let the wild rumpus begin!" Also, staring—in a riveting, mesmerizing manner. According to the book, the wildest thing of all is what Max accomplished with his eyes as he LOOKED at the wild things: "staring into all their yellow eyes without blinking once." I have been on the receiving end of that kind of stare as I have gazed at Silky's wild face and been transfixed by the same big, round, bright yellow eyes that we see on Sendak's wild things; it dazzles you, making you freeze in your tracks.

Do the wild things have something of us in them? The images of Sendak's wild things have a wide range of human, refined, and expressive looks on their faces. And for Pete's sake, look at the feet on the bull-like creature. On the other hand, do we have something of the "wild thing" in us? Or is it just one big ball of wax? Should I even be trying to think of "us" and "them" in separate categories? Interestingly, children often anthropomorphize in their portrayal of animals. They easily accept the notion of animals wearing clothing, or walking upright on hind legs, or even carrying umbrellas for protection from the rain!

Max does go about trying to tame the wild things, or to control them, but only so that he can be their king. And he does it with the aforementioned wildest thing of all—staring.

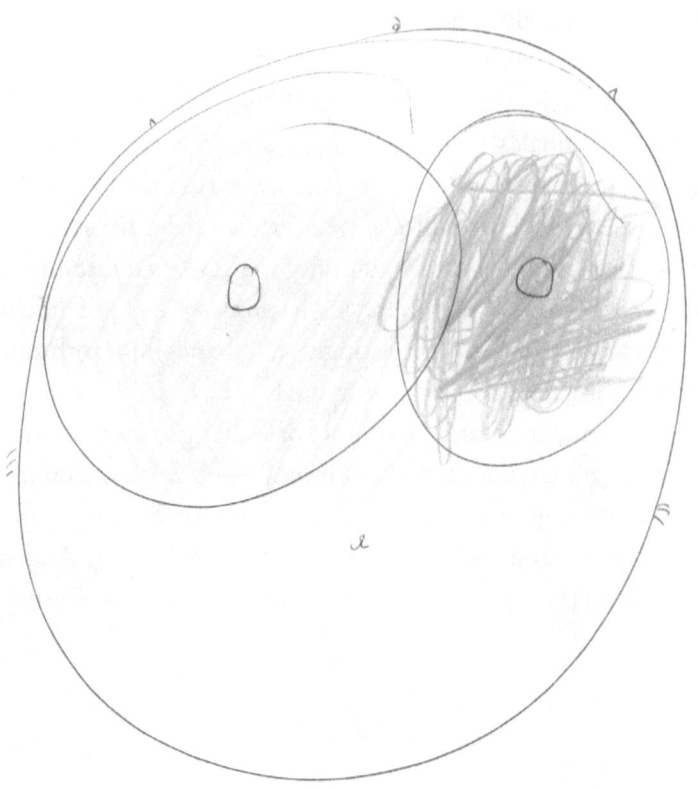

Do we want to capture wildness, thus to restrain, subdue, or banish it? I think not. Because surely there are important elements of "wildness" that we need to hang on to—that we probably will hang on to. Do we want to "capture" childhood (thereby to restrain, subdue, or banish it) and grow up to achieve complete and absolute "maturity" (whatever that is)?

"It's nice to grow up without being entirely grown-up."

"Maturity is finding out you're just like everyone else."

Who wants the latter? I think no one!

Patient and faithful reader, I remind you again how I felt at the beginning of this story when I realized I had captured wild Silky inside the cage: frightened, deeply troubled, discomposed, like the world around me was coming to an end. There was definitely, and surprisingly, a feeling of doom! *Should I have done this?* I wondered. Let us remember, too, in the epigraph for the end of Part One, the "sleek, wild, dark and iridescent creature" trapped and desperate inside the house in Richard Wilbur's poem *The Writer*: "How our spirits rose when, suddenly sure, it lifted off from a chair-back, beating a smooth course for the right window and clearing the sill of the world." Free at last.

Thoreau said, "In wildness is the preservation of the world."[24] But in *The Little Prince*, Antoine de Saint-Exupéry wrote, "The only things you learn are the things you tame," referring to the relationship between the prince and his rose growing on his home planet, Asteroid B-612.[25] So we have a dichotomy here. Thoreau expresses it so well: "At the same time that we are earnest to explore and learn all things, we require that all things be mysterious and unexplorable, that land and sea be infinitely wild, unsurveyed and unfathomed by us because unfathomable."[26]

* * *

There is a conversation relevant to this story that takes place within the pages of *The Little Prince*. Having recently arrived on Earth from the very small planet known in the book as Asteroid B-612, the young prince wants to know what trains

---

[24] Thoreau, "Walking."
[25] Antoine de Saint-Exupéry (translated by Richard Howard), *The Little Prince* (New York: Clarion Books, 2000).
[26] Thoreau, *Walden*.

are for, what they do, and what goes on inside them. "Are the travelers on one train chasing the travelers on another train?" he asks.

"The travelers are not chasing anything," the railway switchman replies, "They're sleeping in there, or else they're yawning. Only the children are pressing their noses against the windowpanes."[27]

This is a perfect example of "embracing the journey," one of the themes of my story.

* * *

Will I do anything about Silky's possible bug problem? I don't know. The life of a wild thing isn't easy, and at the same time, perhaps isn't meant to be. I need to accept that and perhaps just "let her go." Let Nature take its course and don't interfere. I don't know if I'm happy with this plan of action—or rather nonaction.

* * *

In this rural countryside patchwork of many farms, there are lots of orchards. Right outside my home, there are robust apple trees, a couple of giant pear trees, and a number of much smaller, and somewhat struggling, old peach trees. The abundant apples are now starting to turn red. Maybe Silky should eat apples. I'm not aware that she does eat this fine fruit.

Silky should try consuming less raw animal carcass and more fresh fruit. Don't you think? Maybe she is already trying this. Seems to me apples would do a good job of cleaning her teeth. And how about the delicious and diverse flavors of

---

[27] Saint-Exupéry, *The Little Prince.*

those dangling delights? And the shape! Cats like round, ball-like objects, right? They like to play with such. Wouldn't it be fun to bat an apple back and forth between paws or play chase with it? Do feral cats play?

Experts undoubtedly have answers to these questions. But I don't see the harm in trying things. And certainly, there's no harm in sitting here staring out the window and wondering.

Saturday, August 3, 2013

Tonight, I drove by my workplace on my way home from taking in an art exhibit in a small city some distance away. It was late and I was hungry—I had purchased my supper on the way home, and it was with me in my car, waiting to be devoured within minutes. It was a beautiful night, dark, with clouds only slowly clearing after a day of intermittent rain so that the earth and atmosphere had a cool, refreshed, still-moist feeling, my outlook framed by suggestions of lurking, light, vaguely luminous fog.

I glanced up the small rise to the parking lot of my workplace. It was lit by the lot lamps, and looked lonely and deserted and ever so quiet. But I knew by now that the entire area pulsed with life-forms (half of which I can't even imagine), especially in those places in the deep shadows and hidden from full view. In fact, even, different generations existed in a short length of time right here—those being born, growing, aging, and then dying (already replaced by the next generation).

Perhaps they're all hearing, at some point in their lives, the ethereal music of reeds played by the breath of Pan, which announces a visit from him, their Friend and Helper, The Piper at the Gates of Dawn, he who graced the trembling Ratty and Mole with his presence, dazzling them with his music and then revealing and returning to them their lost, floundering, endangered little friend, Portly—the baby otter, now held safe, nestling between his hooves, sleeping soundly in entire peace and contentment.[28] I know by now that all of this occurs while I and my colleagues and the children in our care, oblivious to it, go about our own daily business here.

I saw Cat Haven. I saw location C. I saw the small fleet of big yellow buses parked neatly, side by side. I felt profoundly sad and lonely because I knew I wasn't going to drive up there this particular night and plumb the depths for Silky. And I didn't. *Where is Silky?* I wondered as I drove past. *Is she up there? Searching for Nancy?* If she was up there, she would not find me there tonight. I wouldn't be giving her any help or friendly attention tonight.

If only Silky and I could be together always. I would take care of her, make sure she is healthy and content, purring at my side. Wouldn't we both be happy then?

"I Had a Little Cat" (folk song from Kentucky, the Southern Mountains, USA)

Verse 1
I had a little cat,
And the cat pleased me,
I fed my cat under yonders tree:
Cat goes fiddle-i-fee.[29]

---

[28] (Thus was Portly rescued, saved, protected by the powers that be in *The Wind In The Willows* by Kenneth Grahame.)

[29] John Langstaff, *Gather My Gold Together, Four Songs For Four Seasons* (New York: Doubleday & Co, 1971).

PART THREE

Five Years Later

Portrait of a Cat

Tuesday, May 29, 2018

3:30 p.m.

Having retired from work at the school introduced to you in Chapter 1, and indeed having moved away from that area entirely, I visited the place only occasionally now, to help out by playing the piano or glockenspiel for group singing. That was my role in this day's drama production of *Peter Rabbit*, deftly directed by Mrs. Monamie Géniegékas.

After the final rehearsal of the play, which took place outside in the school's flower and vegetable garden, a small furry face peered out from underneath a nearby sturdy outdoor platform, this platform being the floor of the very "pavilion" envisioned by Mr. King to me back in April 2010. Life goes on. "Kitten!" came the cry. "There's a kitten!" Once the magic word was uttered, an excited crowd quickly gathered to gush and marvel at this sight. It was with difficulty that the Young Performers troupe, and their adult parents, brought their attention back to the play, which finally began around 4:15. But this they did, and with great success.

The "rabbits" rabbited, using eloquent English. "McGregor" ranted and threatened appropriately, and the "sparrows" sparrowed and chattered on cue. The "robin" went bob, bob, bobbin' along, and "Beatrix Potter" told her story with insight and loving humor.

After dismissal, key players in my story lingered, trying to figure out what should be done with the recently discovered, possibly feral, kittens. One particularly skillful habitué of the establishment, Miss Polite, was able to capture the first peeking kitten, the bold one, by the scruff of the neck. This kitten, named Midnight East by one of the fascinated children, snuggled into his captor's arms. A cardboard box was produced and Midnight East placed inside. Much musing, and studying of the situation, ensued. Hours passed. The opinions of experts were sought. Other small furry faces tantalized us from beneath the platform.

Mrs. Danas Myth called Mr. Vet to the scene. Mrs. Myth's daughter Cecilya had been very busy thinking of every possible argument she could use to persuade her father to accept Midnight East into their home as a pet for herself and her sister Nelilya. When Mr. Vet arrived, accompanied by his son Will B. Vet, he handled Midnight East tenderly and expertly and said he was about five weeks old, maybe six, and in good shape—ready to be adopted. Mrs. Vet (no relation to Mr. Vet) was phoned and became part of the discussion remotely. Referring to Midnight East, Mrs. Vet enthused, "This one's a cutie!" It wasn't long before a member of our party, Doña Kañuspella, was seen heading for her car, carefully holding the cardboard box containing the good-looking M.E.

Will B. came up with ingenious suggestions for getting a hold of the siblings of M.E., now lying low and quiet under the platform. However, the equipment he required was not at hand. Mr. Vet felt that the baby kittens closest to the edge of the platform (i.e., in their exit/entry space) might be the healthiest—these wanted to emerge, to be selected, like the first one, Midnight East, the bold one. I wanted to hear more, to understand this concept of "selection" better, but at that point Will B. was expressing at length his strong dislike of crows; this subject was important to the boy, and he spoke about it, obviously from crow experience, with passion and imagination, so that I was drawn in, fascinated, wondering how it might be relevant to the situation in which we found ourselves.

Mr. Vet observed that cats don't need to intake water as often, and as much, as I had thought. Something about cats' history in ancient Egypt . . . and the fact that they evolved from desert dwellers . . .

But it was getting late and time for the Vets to get home, leaving me to ponder their wisdom and ideas in solitude. Keeping watch in the same parking lot as at the beginning of my story, at the very same institution, on the same campus where Silky had birthed her four kittens, Barny, Smoky, Cooky, and Joe. Using the same fixed gaze, with an attitude of growing excitement and hopeful anticipation.

7:00 p.m.

A sleek, sinuous, silk-like yet sinewy cat suddenly appeared on the scene. My first thought was that it was the mother cat, confirmed in short order by the activities that followed. She matched the description of a cat seen often, recently, around the various buildings by various denizens of this campus, reports of which sightings I had heard this afternoon. She moseyed around near the edge of the platform where the excited crowd had gathered earlier. When she had drawn very close to the space from which Midnight East had emerged, one, two, three kittens came out from the hideout to join her—or rather tumble over and around her—as she sat patiently and somewhat aloof, sphinxlike. Finally, she began to feed them.

But suddenly, the roaring of a trash truck bore down on us, shattering our peaceful moment. Mercy me. Monster

Mouth prowled closer and closer, sending the mother cat and her babies diving for cover, which of course was close by. The hungry beast rolled this way and that, then finally turned its back and, with a final piercing shriek, lunged away. The ghastly noise quickly faded to stunned silence.

The uneasy stillness prevailed for a long time, it seemed. Forty-five minutes later, cat and kits calmly came out from under the platform, and the mama cat proceeded to bathe her three remaining babies—one black, one black and white, one dark gray mottled and striped. The little ones then explored the outside rim of their platform, but the immediate section only, keeping close to their entry place. Shortly after, they headed back. The black and white kitten, the last to duck under the platform to safety, was the most evident, the most daring; s/he tried several times to climb up to the top surface of the low platform before rejoining the others underneath it.

Miss Polite, who doesn't pussyfoot around, came back to the scene with a can of cat food. Using this item strategically (also showing much patience and employing furtive, crafty hiding maneuvers), she managed to ambush the dark gray, mottled and striped kitten and place the tiny animal into a large cardboard box, which, thankfully, Mr. Vet had advised me to have ready. After I passed along the special instructions for the care of such a young creature, which I had gleaned from my earlier conversations with our experts, Miss Polite packed all loose ends (which would provide incriminating evidence to King and Bark) into the box, along with Motley, and drove home with her prize.

I walked to my car to leave, trailed doggedly by the mama cat, who was now very interested in me and my vehicle. I drove slowly out of the parking lot, satisfied that the cat family was safe for now—kittens Blacky and B&W with their mama, and Midnight East and Motley in friendly, caring households.

Speaking of friendly, caring households, Mrs. Vet still has Barny and Smoky. Another of Silky's babies is with a family associated with the school after which Barny was named; as mentioned earlier in this tome, the name of this cat has been changed from Cooky to Itty Bitty. The fourth baby in that group went to a technician at the animal facility where Mrs. Vet works.

I would dearly love to see Silky's kittens now. I would love to say to them, "My, how you've grown!" I would love to interact with them, tell them stories about their mother, watch them and admire them, give them special treats.

Mrs. Vet's son Zackitty is well established by now as a "cat" person. And Mrs. Vet thinks certain animals make a strong, and sometimes instantaneous, connection with certain humans—like Barny and Smoky with herself. Ah, to have such a bond with a four-legged, or a wings-of-the-air, or a finned.

The four platform kittens and their mother had been an outstanding group to behold. Their fine coats displayed rich, exquisite colors. They looked healthy and fit, their voices sweet and expressive—a most handsome and attractive family. The striking mama cat was colored in a subtle and elegant manner, sporting a striped coat with a pleasing combination of tan, taupe, beige, and russet. O, terrific tabby-teacher, can you teach us to hear the gossamer, ethereal music made by Pan, announcing the presence of the Piper at the Gates of Dawn, he who is the animals' Friend and Helper? We will listen and be still.

The wind in the willows, the breeze in the reeds, Pan's pipes playing—what marvelous, divine music is this? It means something to the animals. What message, perhaps summons, does it bring?

In Greek mythology, Pan was the god of woods and pastures and patron of shepherds and their flocks. Half man and half goat, he was thought to have a wild, unpredictable nature. Pan has traditionally been associated with wilderness regions, thought to live in caves and on mountain slopes.

I have been trying to interpret the meaning of the way in which John Milton treats Pan and the Biblical shepherds in his early, zealously Christian poem "On the Morning of Christ's Nativity." This poem is famous for its extensive references to (the overthrow of) pagan powers, false gods, and delusive idols. Yes, Milton mentions Pan in the poem, but not lumped in with such juggernauts as Thammuz, Ashtaroth, Moloch, Osiris, Isis, and Typhon (a grisly monster with a hundred dragon heads, desiring supremacy of the cosmos). No, Pan was certainly not in the large group of false gods Milton has trooping off to the netherworld like ghosts when they were faced with the infant Christ. Pan, in essence a "nature spirit," is only mentioned—naturally and sweetly enough—in connection with the shepherds of the Nativity story, which makes perfect sense, after all. While caring for their sheep, of course the shepherds' heads would be full of Pan, now presumably exerting his kindly influence on their pastoral scene, and their shepherdly efforts.

So I imagine that here the shepherds are, either out at their work in the "lawns" (patches of grass, or pasturage, maybe a glade, an open space in the woods) or gathered together informally just before dawn for comparing notes, casual chit-chat, counting their sheep. Maybe they felt the pervasive, utterly tranquil peace that Milton describes as suddenly existing on that occasion—they would attribute such a pastoral and peaceful atmosphere as being the influence of Pan.

So Milton says that perhaps they were exchanging thoughts regarding everyday things like their sheep, their love lives, and Pan. The poet rather unceremoniously declares the thoughts occupying the shepherds' minds to be silly and rustic. Well. I swan, sir, this seems a bit judgy and uncalled-for. But I suppose this could be just an effective poetic setup for the sublime and glorious, profoundly consequential event Milton has in mind to introduce as such.

We recognize Pan as the merry music maker of William Blake's poem "Piping Down the Valleys Wild." After all, he is traipsing about in the wilds, piping songs about lambs, and composing happy melodies with a "rural pen" he made from "a hollow reed."

* * *

Wilderness holds beautiful music. It produces beautiful and powerful music. Can we create it? No, but we can hear it, listen to it.

It doesn't get much wilder than the island in Shakespeare's *The Tempest*. Caliban, the beastly, earthy, infamous, and much-maligned character who is the son of a witch-hag, is also the only true native of the island to appear in the play. He is intimately familiar with the natural environment of the island; he values it, he appreciates it, and he is proud of it. He speaks of the "qualities o' the isle, the fresh springs, brine-pits, barren place and fertile." He knows the "bogs, fens, flats." He knows where to pluck berries, to fish, and to find wood. He knows where there are "crabs" (crabapple trees), where to dig for "pig-nuts," where there is a "jay's nest," how to "snare the nimble marmoset," where there are "clustering filberts" and where to find "young scamels from the rock."

Caliban describes the music that emanates from the island's natural environment:

> Be not afeard; the isle is full of noises,
> Sounds and sweet airs, that give delight and hurt not.
> Sometimes a thousand twangling instruments
> Will hum about mine ears, and sometime voices
> That, if I then had waked after long sleep,
> Will make me sleep again: and then, in dreaming,
> The clouds methought would open and show riches
> Ready to drop upon me that, when I waked,
> I cried to dream again.[30]

There is a voice of the wilderness, of the wild state of things. What is this voice? What is it saying? There is a call in it. It will help us.

The call of Spring is a universal sensation, and, like all of ethereal Nature, does not come without its own special music. It's about eternal early morning, the Green Man, the fountain of youth, the unfallen state, Peter Pan, and the harmony of the spheres. Powerful, to be heard and appreciated.

---

[30] From Shakespeare's *The Tempest*, Act III, Scene II, poets.org, accessed September 21, 2024, https://poets.org/poem/tempest-act-iii-scene-ii-be-not-afeard.

It's the sound of Pan, "the goat-footed balloon man," as he "whistles far and wee" in the E. E. Cummings poem "In Just-Spring." Children and Spring. Pan, the Piper at the Gates of Dawn, writing his happy songs "every child may joy to hear" (William Blake, "The Piper"). Here is wildness!

Thoreau put it this way: "I long for wildness, a nature which I cannot put my foot through, woods where the wood thrush forever sings, where the hours are early morning ones, and there is dew on the grass, and the day is forever unproved."[31]

And my reader will have noted that "Pippa's Song," where "All's right with the world," kept entering my mind while experiencing my search for Silky. In this poem, Robert Browning says that all's right with the world because God's in his heaven, the snail's on the thorn, the lark's on the wing, the hillside's dew-pearled, the day's at the morn, and the year's at the spring. Morning. Spring. I believe Browning's words represent the state of wildness, and that the poet feels that this element of wildness is essential to us and to the well-being of our world.

In 1969, Guru Sri Swami Satchidananda opened the Woodstock festival in Bethel, New York, with a blessing beginning with the following words:

> My Beloved Sisters and Brothers: I am overwhelmed with joy to see the entire youth of America gathered here in the name of the fine art of music. In fact, through the music, we can work wonders. Music is a celestial sound and it is the sound that controls the whole universe, not atomic vibrations. Sound

---

[31] Thoreau, *Walden.*

energy, sound power, is much, much greater than any other power in this world . . .[32]

And, continuing to sit cross-legged onstage, he added: "So I am very happy to see that we are all here gathered to create some sounds—to find that peace and joy through the celestial music." And further on, he said, "Through that sacred art of music, let us find peace that will pervade all over the globe."

Read that again: "Through that sacred art of music, let us find peace that will pervade all over the globe."

The swami then led the assembled multitudes in a chant using the ancient Indian language of Sanskrit: "Hari Om, Hari Om, Hari Hari Hari Om . . . Hari Om, Hari Om, Hari Hari Om . . . Rama Rama Rama Rama Rama Rama Rama Ram."

So the guru took the notion of "universal music" a little farther that day, suggesting that we can tap into this celestial music/sound power somehow, and, using it, actually produce, bring about, a positive state of affairs: peace, regeneration, healing, and growth.

Come, wildness—come to me. Always I crave your voice, your music, your tonic.

"This stillness, solitude, wildness of nature is a kind of thoroughwort, or boneset, to my intellect. This is what I go out to seek. It is as if I always met in those places some grand, serene, immortal, infinitely encouraging, though invisible, companion, and walked with him."[33]

---

[32] LIFE editors, *LIFE Woodstock at 50*, single-issue (New York: Meredith Corporation, 2019).
[33] Thoreau, *Walden*.

Searching for Silky is searching for wildness—I yearn for this. I need to find Silky. Maybe she will find me, and I will walk with her. We will walk together.

"The Piper"
by William Blake

Piping down the valleys wild,
    Piping songs of pleasant glee,
On a cloud I saw a child,
    And he laughing said to me:

"Pipe a song about a Lamb!"
    So I piped with merry cheer.
"Piper, pipe that song again";
    So I piped; he wept to hear.

"Drop thy pipe, thy happy pipe;
    Sing thy songs of happy cheer!"
So I sang the same again,
    While he wept with joy to hear.

"Piper, sit thee down and write
    In a book, that all may read."
So he vanished from my sight;
    And I plucked a hollow reed,

And I made a rural pen,
    And I stained the water clear

And I write my happy songs
   Every child may joy to hear.[34]

[34] Edited by Nancy Larrick, *Piping Down the Valleys Wild* (New York: Yearling/Bantam Doubleday Dell Books for Young Readers, 1999).